Seven Keys to Beautify the Overly Aggressive to Become a Virtue Honeybee Lady

Release the Honey within You

Virtue Honeybee Lady

Copyright © 2023 Shantay Adams

Published by Krystal Lee Enterprises LLC (KLE Publishing)
All rights reserved. No parts of this book may be reproduced, distributed, or used in any manner, including photocopying, recording, or other electronic or mechanical methods without the prior written permission of the copywriter owner, except for the use of brief quotations in a book review and certain noncommercial uses permitted by copyright law.

Paperback: 978-1-945066-36-8
All rights reserved. lease send comments and questions:
Krystal Lee Enterprises
sales@KLEPub.com

To Reach the Author:
Email: freshnewconsulting@gmail.com
Web:ShantayAdams.com   Media: @shantayladams
FB Group: Virtue Honeybee Lady Group

Printed in the United States of America.
Disclaimers

The information in this book was correct at the time of publication, but the Author does not assume any liability for loss or damage caused by errors or omissions. These are my memories, from my perspective, and

I have tried to represent events as faithfully as possible.

Dedication

I would like to dedicate this book to my children and my mom.

Table of Contents

Introduction.. 7

Chapter 1
    Valuable..15

Chapter 2
    Identity...29

Chapter 3
    Restoration...49

Chapter 4
    Tactful...65

Chapter 5
    Unstoppable...79

Chapter 6
    Excellence...95

Chapter 7
    Serve..111

Affirmations...125

About the Author
    Shantay Adams...131

Introduction

I was not always a woman with a balanced attitude and perspective on life. If I had to be honest, I was an overly aggressive female on a mission to prove my abilities, skillset, and confirm my ideals about myself. Maybe you share some similarities to me? What kind of woman are you exactly right now, could you speak honestly? Are you kind, loving, understanding, and open minded?

Or, would many describe you as controlling, objective, has to have it your way or no way? Are you more of a spoiled person in people's eyes–that are truthful with you? Would you say you have the ability to own your mistakes and give people room to have grace who need it? Or are you hyper critical of a person's attempt to please and work with you?

Introduction

When you fully embrace the truth, you are becoming a Virtue Honeybee Lady. Virtue is nature, character, strength, moral goodness, moral values, and power. Honeybees naturally are one of the most well-known and economically beneficial insects. Bees produce honey and are very important to our environment by helping with pollination.

They are family oriented and their ability to have a surplus production and storage of honey is well documented. These buzzing creatures are also known for their construction of perennial colonial nests from wax. According to AnimalCorner.org, honeybees are social insects. They have five eyes and have been producing honey for over 100 million years! The Queen honeybee is the only female with fully developed ovaries and the duty of producing chemical scents that help regulate the unity of the colony and laying eggs.

In addition, Queen honeybees control and determine if an egg is fertilized or unfertilized. If fertilized, that honeybee will either become a Worker or another Queen, but if unfertilized that bee will become a male or a drone honeybee. In our environment, bees help flowers to reproduce by transferring pollen from one flower to another flower. If this process was not done, flowers would not have the ability to procreate and would die.

Our beautiful bouquets would not exist nor their scents, colors, and benefits. We benefit greatly from bees helping flowers to reproduce by way of growing beautiful flower gardens. When the honeybee extracts nectar with the pollen from the flower, honey is produced. Honeybees are highly productive and excellent rhythmic communicators when talking to one another. Their dancing is actually a form of communication to others in their colony and as a result, they direct honeybee workers to visit certain flowers and maximize pollination.

Interesting fact, honeybees do not go out looking for trouble, they only sting humans or animals in defense of themselves or their hives. In a lot of ways, being a lady can be likened to a honeybee. Honeybees are valuable to our environment no matter what part of the world you live in. We are queens but it comes with a great deal of responsibility and duties to uphold. It took me a few years after my divorce to be ready to receive and walk in the value within me that is liken unto a honeybee.

If you have gone through a divorce, you probably can relate to being both the father and mother when the other parent is no longer full-time in the home. I have four children all together one is in heaven, my oldest daughter Faith. My two boys are Isaiah and Israel, and then my two grandbabies Heavenly and Khaire. My two boys were by my ex-husband who is active in their lives, but after the divorce I was the one full-time in their daily lives. I had to be the nurturer and the discipliner. Trying to be both roles is very challenging to say the least.

One day I was the nurturer the next day or moment, I had to be the authoritative. In a society where women have joined the workforce, stepped into higher leadership roles, and one day will be madame president confirms the changing role of women in society. (I think it would be wonderful to see a woman as president to demonstrate we have overcome the issue of gender discrimination and sexism.) Over the last few decades and particu-

Introduction

larly the last few years I have noticed a growing trend of some women taking on more masculine characteristics by becoming more aggressive, harder, and domineering in their speech, tone, presentation, and body language. This trend I observed from women in leadership across many business lines in the marketplace, churches, business, entrepreneurship, and non-profit sector.

Again, the reason why I can quickly identify this type of woman is because I used to be her. I grew up with two parents in the household until my father and my mother parted ways when I was 15-years-old. My mother became a full-time parent, and although my father was still an active parent in our lives who loved his children and he was there for us until he transitioned to heaven on March 20, 2022, it was nonetheless different. Watching my mother be both the mom and the dad during that time to my three brothers, sister, and myself was not a walk in the park despite her making it look easy.

She loves her children deeply, but she did not play!. When laying down the law, she could back it up if needed with any one of us! She became more aggressive, harder at times, and assertive in her speech and tone when raising us in an effort to keep us in line. As a 15-year-old girl who observed everything, I learned this behavior. By the time I got married that behavior and cultural influence came with me when I said I do at the age of 28. Sadly, that attitude was still with me when I divorced at 32 years old.

Although I was the one that filed for divorce, I can honestly say two things: I was not ready for marriage at that time and I poured out more vinegar than honey. Now eight years later, one of my favorite quotes to say is, "You get more with honey than vinegar." My ex-husband said that quote to me often when we were married. I did not realize all the vinegar I poured out of my mouth and the over dominating behavior was not good nor beneficial. How I overcame being the old me patterned by upbringing and culture to be more aggressive for protection had to be shifted by having open heart surgery.

Open Heart Surgery

Now, moving past the stage of preparation for surgery, I had to get rid of the junk and dead weight saddled to my heart. The way I thought, responded, and behaved had to be renewed to save my life. When I began the venture of really loving and valuing myself, I clearly saw I had ways about myself that were toxic and not healthy. A Lot of that toughness I displayed came from a place of some bitterness and a whole lot of brokenness.

During this great deliverance and open heart surgery, those issues in my heart were coming out little by little including low self-esteem and insecurities which we will talk more about in the next chapter, "Identity." I was off balance as a woman and I was more of a bee than a virtue honeybee. Allow me to further explain, I was feisty and ready for a fight. I grew up in humble beginnings and surrounded by gangs. The softer side and showing affection was not always easy for me.

In my household as a child growing up we did not show daily affection to one another even though we loved each other. The harder exterior followed me in my career. When it was revealed to me in my quiet time, I began to

Introduction

seek and ask the Creator who created me to help me become more softer and balanced in every way. There were some areas where I was soft, but I lacked consistency. Once those unfruitful and imbalanced ways were taken out of me during my years of open heart surgery, it was replaced with the honey of a balanced soft, gentle, and calm nature.

A Virtue Honeybee Lady is a type of lady that is balanced in her character. She is sweet, kind-hearted, loving, humble, while simultaneously being firm, strong, bold, powerful, courageous, vigorous, sharp, unbreakable, and unstoppable. She is a force to be reckoned with in modern day society because she knows who she is and she does not have to change her original design in order to succeed. We as ladies do not need to stop being sharp and savvy, but we must incorporate a consistent steady diet of being sweet like honey. As such, we must be able to sting like a Queen bee toward anyone that will try to attack us or those whom we love or are called to lead.

To provide clarity, I do not mean stinging by taking matters in your own hands, but we will stand up and speak out against injustice. Self-reflection is important at this stage and being honest with yourself. If not, it will affect every area of your life if you forsake taking out the necessary time on the inner self work. The world may say beauty is first on the outward appearance, but I beg a difference, beauty begins from the inward to the outward.

There was a time in my life I was more focused on the outer me in terms of my appearance than the inward me did not get the same attention. The attention I learned to give the inner me, produced a more beautiful me. Over time I was becoming beautified and the inner beauty began to manifest outwardly in every area of my life. No real man that is healed and whole wants a woman that is beautiful on the outside, but when she opens her mouth all that comes out is vinegar. Being virtuous and eating honey is the key.

Honey is the necessary ingredient to having a healthy life, healthy relationships, healthy marriage, healthy career, healthy business, healthy household, healthy ministry, and for raising a healthy generation of ladies and daughters that are coming behind us. The Virtue Honeybee lady is valuable and has worth, she is needed in our environment, society, culture, business, government, education system, family, media, arts, entertainment, and in churches. I recalled my children who are spreaded out in age. My daughter will be 23 years old this year, my oldest son will be 17, and my youngest son is 10. They jokingly talk about the type of mother they received during different phases of their lives.

A Virtue Honeybee Lady has a purpose and is born to release the honey within her to love her family, be successful in her work environment, lead others by starting with herself, and leaving a legacy that expands generations. Turn the page, and let me show you how I started my journey and engaged in conversations that were must-haves to become my best self.

Introduction

Chapter 1 Valuable

*An excellent woman, one who is spiritual, capable, intelligent, and virtuous, who is he who can't find her? Her **value** is more precious than jewels in her words as far above rubies and pearls.* (Proverbs 31:10 AMP)

Value in the sense of being valuable , I did not truly discover and learn until after my divorce. My ex-husband and I divorced on June 19, 2015, less than a year after moving our family to Cincinnati, OH. I remembered like it was yesterday the challenges I began to experience after our divorce. Situations never presented before, manifested, and most were not expected. My life felt like it went upside down in a way that was difficult for me. My ex-husband's mother, whom I loved and honored dearly before she transitioned, said to me after the divorce, "Baby, you are about to go through the school of

Chapter 1 Valuable

a hard-knock life."

As I listened, I knew she meant what she said, but I did not know the magnitude of the transformation process, the reconstruction of my current mindset, views, understanding, behavior, and heart. I was getting ready for a massive heart surgery emotionally and spiritually. She spoke accurately to me but I did not understand the magnitude at the time.

I did not know the journey or venture I should say she spoke of. Based on this working definition of the venture, it is a tailor-made experience that is unique and it can be an exciting, risky, daring, journey to undertake depending on the perspective. The venture began with me preparing for surgery which led to me discovering and learning my worth and value. I was loaded with value and worth before I exited my mother's womb, but I did not fully know nor understand what was already inside me.

The same is true for you reading this book. When you were created, you were loaded with value and worth that was placed inside of you before you came out of your mother's womb. It has been affirmed, sustained, and validated, by the One who is the Creator & Maker. These essential ingredients need to be nurtured and cultivated from childhood to adulthood. Truly knowing and understanding your value and worth are keys to helping us as ladies become valuable. We have something to bring to the table that is not purchased, fabricated, duplicated, or stolen, but it comes from within our DNA. Being valuable is who we are because it is our original design.

Shantay Adams

Being fully enrolled in the school of hard knock life, my first class is called preparation for surgery. The first class was filled with needed details for how to become more intimate and build a deeper relationship with the One who caused all things to exist. He placed value, love, and worth inside of me as He did for you. As I begin to learn my value, worth, I took a deeper dive into loving myself. Remember whatever you feed is what will be cultivated and displayed through you. When I grow in loving myself, slowly but surely transformation starts to take place in my mind and behavior as a person.

We are commanded to love our neighbor as we love ourselves. We are to treat others how we want to be treated also. Many times we want to receive and give out love, but we have not loved and valued ourselves in the proper way. There were relationships I entertained in the past that I knew were not good for me. Growing up I was attracted to what I considered to be *pretty boys* that had some street knowledge, but those relationships did not work out. I am not saying all who share this story cannot have a successful relationship, but chose one who is delivered, healed, & whole.

Some of my relationships I had an inclination in the beginning that they would not be successful, but I still allowed the relationship to go forth until it ended. If I had cultivated love, value, worth, and healthy esteem of myself those dead-end relationships would not have occurred. Looking back I am glad it happened because it eventually led me on an adventure of re-discovering myself and walking in the values that are inside of me. Now I have the opportunity to help other ladies know they are valuable and I can guide them in ways to release

Chapter 1 Valuable

the honey within them.

Ladies, you have value to display consistently in your home, workplace, business, board meetings, during brunch with friends, among colleagues, or if you are out on a date. Boldly and courageously display your values and do not leave them at home. I've read in an iconic book that her value is more precious than jewels and her worth is far above rubies and pearls. Sis, you are a beautiful lady inside and out. The precious value and worth placed within you is far exceedingly greater than rubies, pearls, and the finest jewelry in the world.

My daughter did not receive the fully transformed mom until a few years ago when she moved into her own place. Therefore, most of her life, she experienced the more aggressive and imbalanced mom. My boys on the other hand got to witness a little more of my transformation up close because they were in the same house. They saw my mindset changed for the better, heart attitude, and behavior. Now all of my children and grandchildren are experiencing the Virtue Honeybee mom! If you want to be the better version of yourself it does require consistent work, a commitment to loving yourself, and a desire to show up for you and your children or your future children.

Recently, I attended an event for Coaches, Consulting, Speakers, and Thought Leader, and during the event, the host, Dr. Sonja Stribling asked each of us to close our eyes and picture our current self at our favorite place. My favorite places were the beach sitting on sand and sitting under a date palm tree. As I focused my attention on the beach, I could see the waves of the ocean. Next, while our eyes were still closed, we were told someone is approaching us and that person is the future you.

My future self came to tell and show the present me what is to come in the future. As I imagined this, my future self grabbed my hand and we walked onto a stage. All I could see were people from one side of the stadium to the other side smiling and delighted to see me before I spoke a word. I was there and sent to speak to them as the keynote speaker. My future self was encouraging the present me by reminding me not to give up because life is bigger and abundantly blessed in the future. The future self said to the present, 'keep stepping into the future that is awaiting me. On the other side, there are people waiting on me and I am called to effectively impact and influence positively.

During this exercise, I cried like a baby because it felt so real to me. After I returned back home, just over two weeks later to my surprise, I was contacted to be a speaker at the WYN Conference in New York City, for their Fourth Annual International Ultimate Congress of Women Expo 2023, the theme is *New Insights into the function of Women Leadership.* I was in awe of the amazing invitation and it was an honor and privilege. I accepted the invitation and began preparing myself to be a public International Speaker.
You, beautiful lady, who is reading this book, your future self is nearby encouraging and welcoming you to embrace this part of your life to become a Virtue Honeybee Lady. This is a friendly reminder to the future you and all those you are called to impact, and influence is waiting on you so keep pressing forward. Keep going forward and do not shrink back in fear and retreat to the place

Chapter 1 Valuable

of familiarity. The place of familiarity is also a comfort zone. We are not called to stay still in one place with no growth, but to increase and expand .

Our future self comes to let us know to continue to grow and develop, take risks, evolve, and keep an open heart and mind. The Virtue Honeybee Lady is fabulous, she is healed, whole, intelligent, full of life, joy and peace. She is vibrant, prosperous, successful, confident, creative, and a lady of excellence. These ladies are caregivers, a help met, brilliant, and have integrity. She is courageous, bold, fearless, brave, and beautiful inside and out.

But she is more of a lover, not a hater. She does not compete with other ladies only herself, and she is a savvy leader in the home, church, marketplace, and business. She is not just a conqueror, but she is an overcomer. She is a team player, a strategist and a problem-solver. This lady has power and is clothed in strength and dignity. She brings her tenacious personality, grit, audacious and noble heart everywhere she goes. She walks in honor and pours out honor like a drink offering. Lastly, she has substance and value to offer in any circumstance.

The Virtue Queen Honeybee Lady's name proceeds her in rooms she has not yet entered. She operates with decency and pure motives. Her honesty is well known, and she is known to be a leader of her word. Her mouth will speak excellent, kind, and noble things because her heart is pure and full of honey. My child, eat the honey, for it is good and a honeycomb is sweet to the taste. In the same way, wisdom is sweet to the soul. If you find it, you will have a bright future, and your hopes will not be cut short. (Proverbs 24:13-14 NLT).

Another element in the open heart surgery stage was unlearning certain ways about myself that were not beneficial to me and others. I had to unlearn how I viewed myself, parenting, relationship, communication, and leadership. I stated earlier, my daughter growing up experienced a different kind of mother. I was a 17-year-old teenage mom with limited experiences in comparison to the new and improved transformed mom. I was "ma" (as she would say) who was quick tempered and kept an attitude. I had to grow up because I was passing down those character traits to my daughter, my next generation.

No one knows exactly how to parent a child until stepping into those the shoes. We have examples around us that may include our parents, family, friends, first-time parent books provide tips and tools on a general basis. Nowadays, some people turn to various social or media outlets for advice. All the education that is available, nothing compares to on the job training parents experience when raising their children. I believe many parents would agree, no two children are alike; and other people's children, or your children around others can act differently.

As parents, we go over the bumps on the road trying to figure things out especially if the parent or child's personality is different. For example, if one is more outgoing and enjoys the company of others, and the other is quiet and prefers to be to himself or herself this creates a learning curve. This challenge occurs often in parenting and we learn to figure it out to have a healthy and loving relationship with our children. If I did not receive deliverance, become more balanced, healed and whole, the overly feistiness in my gas tank would have ruined

Chapter 1 Valuable

my relationship with my children, particularly with my daughter because we bumped heads quite a bit.

During the time when I was overly feisty and overly aggressive, I was creating a cultural norm which was causing my daughter to develop unfruitful ways that would not benefit her in the long term. In addition, it would weaken our mother daughter bond. Women who are overly feisty and or overly aggressive may get a pass here and there from people because some may consider the behavior to be cute or funny. However, over time if the woman does not manage and operate with both ingredients of self-control and honey, the relationship may come to an end prematurely. Making the decision to show up better for myself has created a domino effect for every area of my life including being a better parent and leader.

Embracing healthier ways helped me to accomplish great results and success. As a disclaimer, a healthier way does not mean I was more lenient or not as stern when needed, but I learned when to be more soft and gentle in my approach rather than the one who would shoot first then ask questions later. I learned to be soft and savvy. The attributes and character of virtue includes excellence, nobleness, strength, power, responsibility, decency, honor, integrity, moral goodness, and rectitude; those qualities began to shape the way I carried myself. My value system was updated which caused me to become more valuable.

I encourage you to let the character of virtue take root in your heart and behavior for it will produce great success for you. Especially in the area of relationship with the opposite sex. Recently, I had a conversation with a male friend of mine who is single and he is successful in his leadership position as the Director. We had a conversation about women that were more aggressive in their approach, posture, interaction, and speech. He shared he did not find that appealing for a long term relationship or marriage. One thing I have learned about a healed and whole man or a man in pursuit of it, he wants a lady that does not only know when to be soft, but is soft and sweet like honey.

He does not want to come home to a woman or his wife that is overbarrening, wanting to dominate, control, or is overly assertive toward him with her mouth, attitude, and behavior. There is a difference between a woman and a lady. Little girls grow up to be women, but not all women become and conduct themselves as ladies. As a child growing up, my mother raised me to be ladylike, but in my teenage years once my father was no longer in the home, I was less ladylike. When I began to walk in life personally and professionally as a lady again, I learned I was more valuable and it was key to a prosperous life.

Once the mystery was unlocked to me, everything about me shifted quickly. As ladies we have something to offer of value, we should no longer have the need or desire to over assert ourselves to be heard. Nor should we try to dominate a situation to show we are powerful or we can do what men do to validate ourselves. When value is fully present and in full operation in your life, it will speak for you and proceed you in rooms, spaces, and places your feet have yet to enter. A lady has value and she is valuable and is irreplaceable. There is no denying she has value worth keeping.

Chapter 1 Valuable

I want to show you that becoming a Virtue Honeybee Lady makes you an asset to your husband (or future husband), your family, career, relationships, business, your community, city, region, and nation. Her purpose in life is to become unstoppable. As I continued my conversation with my friend who coined this conversation as women's masculinity, he stated, "It is more prevalent in this generation in my opinion. It felt like more of a single minority women issue prior, but now that women are established in high-ranking positions in the workplace it's become common among all women that want to make it in business. They think it's necessary in order to compete and manage men."

He spoke from the perspective of women in the marketplace, but I would add this type of tact and mindset has spilled over to our household culture, relationship with the opposite sex, and it is influencing and conditioning the current and next generation of ladies and leaders. Society, particularly in arenas where men have dominated, have tried to silence women, put them in a corner, or block them from advancing to the next level professionally, and getting equal pay played a role in this adaptive behavior. These types of hindrances are never appropriate and are flat out wrong.

Women have responded more assertively because they felt like they did not have a choice. They wanted to speak up against injustice and discrimination. I agree women should continue to be in positions of leadership with equal pay for equal work. According to Pew Research Center, women earned an average of 82% of what men earned in 2022. The feminist movement was great with creating equal opportunities, achieving full gender equality, and new freedoms for women to end discrimination, sexism, and violence by pursuing social and legal reform. However, in the spirit of *I am an independent woman, I do not need a man, I can do what men do and even better, I will compete with men and other women if need be to prove I am strong and not weak.* This thought process has condition, trained, inspired, and birth overly aggressive behavior, tone, attitude, and speech.

The unhealthiness of this behavior has caused marital issues, divorce, and some never have been married. Some people only get to be engaged, but many find it difficult to get or have a successful courtship. Most if not all healthy healed and whole men are walking and living out their divine purpose are successful and want a helper who is soft and savvy. The Virtue Honeybee Lady is a strong, powerful, humble yet confident, fearless, bold, resilient, resolute, courageous, calm, modest, and savvy as she walks in her femininity with pearls of wisdom. She understands a patient and calm spirit can persuade kings and a soft and gentle tongue breaks the bone of resistance. (see Proverbs 25:11 AMP)

I am a witness and I have personal experience to know this is true. When I began to apply the principle of this truth everything about me began to radically change. The softer side I needed, desired, and sought after began to bear fruit in my life as evidence that honey was added to my daily diet. I found myself becoming beautified and more effective and successful in life and leadership. Once the surgery stage began I became healed and worked toward becoming whole, due to the cutting away of low self-esteem, fear of failure, roots of rejection, and pride which cater to perfectionism. Afterward, I began

Chapter 1 Valuable

to experience restoration and recovery from surgery as I became healed and whole.

I used to look for acceptance, approval, and validation from men but once surgery was completed and I went through the recovery process, those chains of limitation, hindrance, and self-sabotaging in my life were broken. True freedom became a by-product of my journey's success. It is the marathon of life, no sprints or short cuts. While you are reading this book, utilize it as a self-help guide with keys to help unlock the next level in life, business, career, relationship, leadership, and marriage.

This book will produce greater success, prosperity, sustainability, influence, and effectiveness in your life. All I ask in return, you first make a decision to finish this book, and see it through to the end. The second, give yourself grace to grow, to evolve, and to become a better you. I understand this comes from a person who used to be highly ambitious, a perfectionist, and likely too hard on herself if she made a mistake. However, the venture I embarked on over the past few years has taught me the power of grace and excellence.

If I did not learn to receive and yield to grace in this stage, the old way of thinking and behaving would have tried to return to me, overwhelming me and giving me unnecessary anxiety. But grace and peace stepped in and I was reminded I can be better. I will be better. I will grow and develop into the person I was originally designed to be in this world. Great success was and will be my portion.

Lastly, you remain disciplined with adding honey to your

daily life ingredients. As your guide, I am here to encourage you along the way and provide support, insight, wisdom, clarity, and strategies that have benefited me. I know my truth will benefit you. It is time for your venture to be beautified as a Virtue Queen Honeybee Lady. You can do it, you got this, and remember you are not alone. Let's be the change we want to see in this world, in our sphere of influence, and be distinguished and distinct.

At the end of each chapter recite the declarations and on page 123, you will find all declarations included in this book. Please feel free to read them at any time and use them as often as you need them. I still recite these declarations over my life and I encourage you to develop and add more as you need.

Chapter 1 Valuable

Declaration for Valuable

I decree and declare as a Virtue Queen Honeybee Lady,

- That will produce honey which is generating success, effectiveness, abundance, wealth, influence, and sustainability in life and leadership.
- I have value and worth inside of me that I bring to the table.
- I walk in Wisdom and Understanding, life, grace, and favor will be with me in my life, household, career, business, and marriage.
- I will empower my generation and the next generation to know they have value and worth inside of them.
- I will be balanced in being soft and savvy.
- I will walk discipline with a daily diet of honey.
- I will start what I finish boldly and courageously.
- That loves and invest in myself. I will grow and evolve into a better version of me.
- I will be an authentic, unique, and distinguished Virtue Honeybee Lady in life and leadership.
- I am brave, virtuous, humble, confident, intelligent, temper, gentle, bold, resilient, resolute, peaceful, wise, beautiful inside and out, calm, strong, excellent, and ladylike.

Chapter 2 Identity

"To receive the fullness of life's blessing we must walk unapologetically clothed in our true authentic identity as a person." Shantay Adams

After my ex-husband and I divorce in 2015 it was a death I experienced the shedding away of the old me. The version of me I thought I was comfortable being here on earth. What was revealed to me when I was by myself and I needed some work. During that time I was enabled to go deeper in reflection and to take inventory of my life.

Have you reached a point where you think you hit rock bottom? At this point of my life I had hit rock bottom emotionally and I went through a humbling process. The journey or as I like to say venture because it sounds

Chapter 2 Identity

more exciting, led to the discovery of my unapologetic true identity. This was challenging for me but an venture I would not take back. It may be challenging for you to look at who you are, the good, bad, and ugly.

I am very grateful for the life experience it has helped make the Virtue HoneyBee Lady I am today. I was an honor roll student and a patrol officer in grade school. Yes, I was a patrol officer that monitored the hallway at my station for those who were tardy. To be in this role you had to be a student that had good grades and good behavior. As a child I liked the attention I received for excellence work academically and morally. The desire did not change when I reached adulthood, but extended well into my professional life and career.

My family thought I would be successful and I relished in the way I was seen by them, my peers, and friends. This outlook had fueled my high achieving ambitious attitude and drove me from within to succeed . My mother nicknamed me Missey because she would say "you *have been here before,*" *and I was a little lady*, who had an *old soul*. She often told me as a child I would not play with toys or dolls but would have a book in my hand reading while sitting on my bed.

There were times I recalled her saying to me, "Missey put the book down and go play outside with your dolls." Eventually, I would play with the dolls and go outside to play. It's funny, I forgot some of those stories until my mom graciously reminded me, but as an adult I still have books on my bed, literally!

I have to admit, being a coach and trainer has come to

Shantay Adams

me naturally. I remember having my siblings be my first studies and I would teach them different things and assign them school work. To make it even more real, I would grade their work when they turned it in. Remaining discipline in terms of my work ethic was in me since I could remember as a child it propelled me to go forward vigorously with determination. Once my mind was made up there was no stopping me as I moved full steam ahead.

Do you have a determined spirit also? Can you make up your mind and keep your focus and attention on that spot, action, or goal? Having the ability to be hyper focused seems to be a dying art with many things flying in our direction on a regular basis. If you have this gift, don't throw it away, but leverage it to work for you.

Growing up, I remembered teachers and people in my neighborhood often associated me with my family once they learned my maiden name was "King." There were moments I was not a fan of being grouped with the other "King's" because there were some who did not have the best reputation as kids and I wanted to set myself apart from them. Being guilty by association was never fun for me and it was something I worked hard to change. I wanted people to see me and know me for me, not for what someone else had done.

People in my neighborhood would say "You look like a King, are you a King?" or "Are you one of those King's from Alexander street." The report I would hear was sometimes good but I preferred for it to never be bad. Teachers would look at me as if I may give them a hard time and I hated that feeling. To be fair, three teachers

Chapter 2 Identity

stick out in my memory vividly and they were my kindergarten, 1st grade, and 2nd grade teachers. They would say, "I was a teacher to your mom and she was a smart student." I determined in my mind I was going to prove them right and be a good student with grades and behavior to reflect it.

I excelled and worked hard to be successful starting as young as kindergarten. Working hard was embedded in me growing up in order to have a successful life and be an independent woman that does not need to depend on anyone. I do believe it is important to work hard, set goals, and execute them. I was never taught to have a healthy balance in life as a whole. I had an imbalance in the way I approached life and my career. I associate my accomplishments and what I had with my identity rather than who I am as my true identity.

The death of my divorce in 2015 caused the beautifying and restoration of a new me. The woman, wife who had a partner and help, at times I didn't fully appreciate if I am being honest, was gone. At the onset I was an independent woman who began an venture of discovering my unapologetic authentic true identity. This was not an immediate change, it took time and it takes time to learn to live without someone.

The first two or three years post divorce was a process of stripping away my old thoughts, co-dependencies, old mindset towards how I saw myself, and how the old me impacted my decision making. I learned for me it was not as much about being in a male dominating society or culture. I discovered going back as early as my childhood I had the wrong understanding of what defines me.

For example, I was one who did not aim for excellence, but instead I aimed for perfectionism.

Everything had to be right or at least appear to be right in my eyes for the outside world to see about me. Perfectionism would keep me up late at night if I had a project to complete. The attention I received from being recognized at work fueled a desire in me to not make mistakes. Making mistakes was embarrassing for me and would eventually wound my heart with disappointment. I conditioned myself to work twice or sometimes three times harder to live up to my expectation of myself.

Honestly speaking, I did not want people to see me make a mistake. At that time, my reputation was building as a highly competitive and high achieving professional. As a competitive person I played basketball, performed in dance competitions and events in the community, and I always wanted to win. The competitive nature was in me from a child into my adulthood not against others but toward myself. There was a deep seated fear of rejection and the fear of failure was not seen to anyone like it was for me.

Fear would manifest itself if I made any type of mistakes including anything work related. Back in those days I was extremely hard on myself, over analyzing everything I said or did to see where the fault lies. Granted, I would do the same thing with other people because I was projecting my mindset on other people. The way you think and operate does impact the people around you both positively and negatively. I was hard on myself. I didn't think twice about being too hard on others.

Chapter 2 Identity

Are you a perfectionist looking to have everything perfect and seeing that trait help make and destroy your life? People that were close to me would say "Why are you so hard on yourself? Do not let the mistake pull you down." Or the famous statement, "Mistakes happen, it is a part of life." I did not realize my ongoing fight from mistakes stemmed from my fear of rejection. It took time post divorce for me to understand, accept, and embrace mistakes as a part of life and it happens to the best of people.

Have you witnessed something about yourself that you are now wanting to revisit and look at deeper? If you are hard on yourself like I was, I want you to ask yourself the question, why? It is important to identify the root cause of your actions because the only way to overcome it is to learn what you are fighting. When I left the reason undiscovered, I noticed it impacted my temper and attitude. I had a bad attitude and a quick temper because I lacked patience.

Lacking patience was related to my desire to overcompensate to avoid making mistakes. I did feel my way was a sure way to avoid failure, I had a lot of practice. The truth, I could still be wrong, which was equivalent to making a mistake. The steps I took to overcome this problem were first changing my mindset. I needed deliverance for how I used to think, make decisions, and the patterns I had created to support my avoidance of making mistakes. I had to take a look at my childhood, revisit conversations and actions I made during my marriage. I had to look at myself before I could correct or overcorrect someone else.

Secondly, I had to learn how to receive grace so I could

give it. I cannot give what I do not have. I had no grace for myself, I could not give to anyone else. I demanded perfection but had to learn that excellent is something we strive for, but we have to be okay with the results being different. Perfect is not always the way you originally intended, sometimes the ending result is better than the vision if you give it room to grow on you.

I worked diligently toward shaking off the dust of any mistake that would occur so I did not put myself in bondage and condemnation. I want you to consider, have you put yourself in emotional, mental, or physical bondage? Is your mindset limiting your life, future, and plans? Noticing I was free when I made a mistake and I did not beat myself up over it was a breakthrough moment. I learned when mistakes occur it is an opportunity to learn the lesson, grow from it, gain and apply wisdom, or appreciate and heed the valuable insight. I made the necessary adjustments or corrections I needed to keep going and stopped reflecting on the negative.

Are you spending too much time thinking about the negative or things you cannot change? Other benefits I learned from making mistakes that would be beneficial to any type A personality: it's okay to make a mistake and it is not the end of the world. You become a better problem solver, critical thinker, and your memory will be improved because you know what not to do again. Finally, I learned failure or mistakes makes success much sweeter like honey!

In terms of the fear of rejection, while in the marketplace or in the church there were insecurities, low self esteem, sadness if not invited to events, or if someone would

Chapter 2 Identity

treat me poorly. I realized I am overly sensitive which many would not believe given my attitude prior. The fear of rejection produced an overly aggressive assertive woman that operated from a place of perfectionism. No one knew I struggled in these areas because I excelled professionally as a leader and I over compensated for those areas that were flawed by accomplishing great work.

The fear of rejection was defeated when I fully received the Love I needed and yielded to the process of loving myself, investing in me, living courageously, and knowing my value and worth. I became more confident and it grew higher over time. There is no fear in love when perfect full grown love expels all fear.

No longer did I need to secretly seek or desire validation, approval, acceptance or condemnation from anyone to fuel my distorted identity of myself. Simply put, love, which is like a honeycomb, helps us walk in our unapologetic, authentic true identity. Once love takes root, growth, increase, blessings, and success in every area will become evident and undeniable. You will find yourself as a lady in leadership, become more productive, balanced, and lighter because unnecessary pressure will be removed from you. We would free ourselves from mental prison and avoid self sabotage.

Accomplishments are NOT Your Identity

What each of us have accomplished or yet to accomplish in life, are only part of our story but it is not our identity in this world. According to Merriam-Webster, identity is the distinguishing character or personality of an individual. According to Dictionary.com, identity is the state of remaining or being the same one under varying conditions. In short, identity is being your true self no matter the circumstances or environment.

I learned over the years there are people that have accomplished a great deal in life, but have no real sense of their true identity and purpose. One can be a jack of all trades but master of none. Separating what you do from who you are is vital if you are a leader in your household, business, ministry, education, organization, or company. According to HOFSTRA University "The most important task any woman can undergo is the process of self identity formation. Female identity formation is critical to the female individual because the way in which she defines herself and what she bases her sense of self upon will ultimately serve as the foundation for her life."

When a lady walks in her true identity unapologetically not only is she liberated but also everyone and everything she influences is impacted for the better. Walking in a room, she carries such a presence, not arrogance or haughtiness, but a confidence of who she is and what she can bring to the table. I have heard some men say a woman should have things to bring to the table. I agree.

A Virtue Queen HoneyBee will bring love, compassion, gentleness, support, favor, effective communication, good collaboration, empathy, be good listeners, balanced, disciplined, critical thinkers, wise, knowledgeable, understanding, intellectual, worthy, and valuable to name a few. I will be remiss if I did not mention the correlation between the male dominating culture in society and the female identity development.

Chapter 2 Identity

I remember distinctly when I was growing up mostly around my brothers and my male cousins. When I would play outside with the boys I would say to myself I can do what they did and even better. The highly competitive nature within me began to swell up and before I knew it, I would boast in my skill set in comparison to their skill set. I had a strong desire to prove myself even if I was a girl. I can do what they did and still be a girly girl sitting with my legs crossed. Society, our upbringing, our way of thinking, our environments have groomed many modern day women to compete, declare their independence, and prove aggressively they are just as good if not better than their male counterparts instead of working together with them.

Ultimately, there are women that want to be in control and prove they can do the job and take care of themselves. As a Virtue Queen Honeybee Lady in this society, I believe ladies should continue to be in a position of leadership, power, prestige, and influence, but I am here to declare let's be balanced with being both soft and savvy in tone and conduct. We do not want to scare the men away by being overly aggressive nor dismissive of who they inherently are. .

Living and walking in your divine identity includes being in touch with your inner self and knowing who you are without seeking approval from others. There is nothing wrong with people encouraging you to be your true authentic unapologetic self. In fact, it is awesome to receive such encouragement because it builds up your confidence. The truth is there is freedom and liberation in walking in your true identity with courage and boldness. I would like to take a moment to encourage you. I want to encourage you to release the pressure of always feeling you have to do more than be yourself in life.

Have you heard of the famous phrase people say, "do you", which means to *do* what's right for you and do not worry what others think about it? I would like to add, be you so you can effectively do you. As Virtue Honeybee ladies we are designed to be a help by doing and being our true selves. I encourage you–I exhort you to not be pressured to live up to anyone's expectations in terms of your identity originated from above.

Beautiful lady who is fearfully and wonderfully made, you now have the duty to carry out that original plan identity "as a natural" born "woman here" on Earth. For the sake of this generation and the next, when many are questioning their identity, please be unapologetically you! I encourage you to begin or continue to fall in love with your unapologetic self, not who the world says or family members say, but who you know yourself to be from within you. No need to be overly critical of yourself, give and receive grace to continue to evolve as a person.

Another benefit to walking in your true identity it will provide clarity in every area. For example, when you know yourself or begin to embrace all of your original design, you avoid making unwise decisions that waste time in your career, household, relationships, marriage, in dating/courtship, finances, education, business, investments, parenting, and in your life in general. It is worth noting when a Virtue Queen HoneyBee lady walks in her true identity and purpose she has no need to be clingy, needed, nor walk or speak in an over aggressive nature.

Chapter 2 Identity

She fully knows and understands she is the good thing, has value, and favor resides with her.

The truth of that statement I did not completely grasp until post divorce, how about you? Did you catch it? I admit I did not fully know Shantay. My identity at one point was associated with my accomplishments, go-getter type A personality, and the independent woman mindset of "hear me roar!" There is nothing wrong with a go-getter type A personality or high achieving ladies who work effectively and efficiently to accomplish and obtain great success in life. Those are beautiful achievements and I rejoice and celebrate with you! The problem only occurs when the independent woman becomes overly aggressive in speech, behavior, and tone resulting in her being out of balance. Honey is the ingredient to cause the weight of the scale to be back balanced and aligned.

The potent sweetness of honey offset and minimizes any propensity to be overly aggressive, assertive, or harsh in her speech or behavior. Instead this added ingredient to the sweet speech increases persuasiveness and learning for the speaker and listener. Virtue Queen Honeybee Ladies are not perceived to be pushy, overbearing, nor heavy-handed because she has the proclivity to be honeyed. A just scale or balance in life helps ensure our success. When we are out of balance we are deficient in one or more areas. This goes back to our decision making especially.

For example, when we do not get proper rest at night it will reduce alertness and awareness, produce poorer judgment, shorten your attention span or aid the lack of focus. Your attitude or mood are impacted and could have the potential to affect how you show up for yourself, spouses, family, colleagues, staff, or business partners. According to the National Heart Lung and Blood Institute, sleep deprivation is a condition that occurs if you don't get enough sleep, sleep at the wrong time of day, or the quality of sleep is poor.

According to the Center for Disease Control and Prevention about 1 in 3 adults in the United States reported not getting enough rest or sleep everyday. That is a lot of people in the grand scheme of things not getting sleep or rest. There is a difference between sleep and rest that is worth mentioning, sleep is critical and vitally important to feeling whole. Yet, sleep is mostly nightly shut eye so the body can recover, refreshed, and renewed. However, on the other hand rest, according to Avent Health, involves your whole being not just your physical body. Complete and proper rest restores your health, enhances your performance and achieves an excellent sense of wellness.

Did you know sleep and rest have a tremendous impact on our bodies and overall life and health. I can honestly admit I have been a person who will stay up late to get work done or accomplish my goal for a task at hand. I worked in Human Resources for over 10 plus years and I have had my fair share of meeting deadlines that extended well beyond my normal 9 to 5 shift. I would pull an all-nighter or work longer days as a result of my driven work ethic. As a result, I would only get so much sleep and I would honestly wake up feeling as if I got no rest at all and it influenced my decision making.

As a woman who was once overly aggressive, I despised not being in control and would sacrifice sleep and

Chapter 2 Identity

sometimes vacation to get work done. However, once I learned and embraced my true identity the sense of control eased and I did not feel the need to be in control because I know who I am and in reality, I am not in complete control of anything in life. If you are in leadership, if you are a business owner, entrepreneur, if you manage teams, you have a reputation to uphold and you want people to always see you in your best light. If you do not get the proper rest that is needed it will impact your life, work performance, and the measure of success you will obtain. An area of breakthrough occurred for me when I began to understand, know, and walk in my true identity.

As a Virtue Queen Honeybee lady everything concerning me shifted for the better as I discovered being my unapologetic self was bigger and more valuable than any accomplishment I have ever obtained. The fruit of success, promotion, elevation, and balance was evident and undeniable and accompanied me being my divine self. Growing up, many of us were taught hard work pays off and some may have worked twice as hard in a male dominated work environment. Many of us ladies were not taken seriously by men even if we accomplished success in our own right. The lack of support has pushed many of us to a place of independence without balance. Now is the time for this generation of ladies and beyond to not feel we have to work twice as hard and over assert ourselves, but rather work smarter not harder.

I want you to vow to become more effective and waste no more time getting to know and be you. With my years in the Human Resources industry, I have heard countless stories of colleagues taking work on vacation only to return and work some more. We must have work-life balance and your personal life should not be a permanent sacrifice for you to succeed. Taking care of yourself is beneficial and it helps the woman that will work and enjoy her life.

Please don't continue to be the woman who struggles internally because of a lack of balance and no self care. Before we can take care of our family, our spouse or significant other, our children, business, our staff, and any ministry commitment or assignment, we must first take care and love ourselves. We cannot pour out we have not placed within. If you are married, your husband needs a present, you. If you are a single mom, your child or your children need a present, you. Lastly, if you are a single lady that desires marriage or companionship, practicing being balanced will help prepare you to receive the man coming into your life. Do not be too busy with your business, ministry, career, or parenting, that you do not recognize him or make time.

For my ladies with a strong work ethic, who are high achieving ladies, allow yourself to be beautified with honey to remove any over-aggression. Allow the soft and supportive side to be shown while demonstrating your

Chapter 2 Identity

strength, resolute, and resilience. You, a Virtue Queen HoneyBee, know what you want and compellingly speak your mind. Don't change that but make better decisions for your health spiritually, emotionally, physically, and mentally. You are not a workhorse, but a woman born with a purpose that expands beyond your type A personality traits.

Recently, I heard a story of a woman who went on a date with a man. She was an independent woman who believed in providing for herself. She did not need nor wanted the man to provide for her on their first date. Her temperament and attitude was revealed when the man reached to pay for the meal. She expressed her displeasure and offense by his actions. The overly aggressive independent woman said, "I can pay for that myself, I don't need a man to take care of me; I am accomplished."

A following week later, that same gentleman went on another date with a different woman and when it was time to pay for the bill the man hesitated. The woman was wondering why he was hesitating, and she thought to herself *if he did not pay for this meal they were not going back on another date.* The man noticed her expression and she communicated her expectation to him to help resolve the awkward moment. These two women had different approaches in the same case, however, they had two different expectations.

The first, may need to adjust her thinking or style of communication if she wants a husband who values taking care and providing for her. She has yet to learn, perhaps, being loved and cared for doesn't rob her of her accomplishments. The second woman was more traditional and yet she had the same level of success as the first lady. You don't have to flaunt your success or change your expectations because you can afford it. She believed men should pay for the meal on the first date and that mindset was how the man was raised.

The first woman was a bee stinging her date without using any honey. Some modern women may want to pay for their date, but the tone and attitude is everything. Instead of going for aggressive and sassy, she could have added honey by saying, "I would like to pay for my meal because I don't want you to feel as if I owe you." Some women like to pay their own way so they can have the right to refuse an offer without guilt. We can talk more about this if you are open to discuss. Please join me on my FB Group Virtue Honeybee Lady to discuss it further.

Being imbalanced in her aggression and independant way of thinking, she did not realize it was perfectly fine to allow the man to pay for their meal. It was also okay for her to be taken care of and to be delicate. One thing to point out, the gentleman in the picture has developed some doubt because the first date went sour instead of sweet. He was left trying to figure out how to approach this dance of paying for the bill when in most cases the man takes the lead.

I do believe most gentlemen respect high achieving and successful women who have been independent for a long time. However, a healed and whole gentleman also wants to lead and take care of the lady in his life. The overly aggressive and independent woman has to become

Chapter 2 Identity

beautified with honey, and step back and allow him to be the gentleman he was originally designed and proposed to be as a provider and protector. In the same breath, ladies we are to be who we were originally designed and purposed to become.

The second lady who is an example of a Virtue Queen Honeybee was balanced in her view of relationships, her identity, and allowing men to be gentlemen. After she effectively communicated and they had a healthy conversation, they got past the bill situation and ultimately went on more dates afterward which became a courtship. Effective communication creates better relationships, builds trust, creates a safe zone, provides clarity, and mitigates conflict. The first date woman did not communicate effectively and her response did not serve her well. As a result, she did not go out on a second date.

Those who are single and desire to be in a healthy monogamous relationship it is important to release honey to be balanced and stay soft. As a lady who has been divorced for several years, I am used to doing a lot of things myself. Small things such as opening the door, bringing in groceries, treating and taking myself out on a date to my favorite restaurant, vacationing are just a few things. I am free to move in my personal life, ministry, finances, and business decisions without consulting anyone. For single ladies who desire marriage, making the necessary adjustments without lowering your standards could lead to marriage.

When two become one, a new identity is established and the successful implementation is required. It becomes the result of two individual glasses of sand coming together in one glass intertwined. To make this work the man must cherish her and be a leader and the lady must honor and respect him as she remains a Virtue Queen Honeybee Lady. Both submitting one to another and honoring their role and identity individually and collectively. If you are in a season of dating, enjoy and embrace your single life, show up as your true unapologetic authentic self but remain balanced. There is no need for a representative because you know that who you are and what you bring to the table is valuable. As you walk as the Virtue Queen Honeybee Lady every area of your life will become better and the evidence of success is produced.

Chapter 2 Identity

Declaration for Identity

I decree and declare as a Virtue Queen Honeybee Lady,

- I will walk in my authentic unapologetic true identity because I am fully acquainted with myself.
- In this world I know who I am and where I am going as I walk purposefully.
- No matter the situation or circumstances, I will walk boldly and courageously in my true self as I was originally designed without shrinking back, but rise to every occasion set before me.
- I will be balanced as being soft and savvy as a Virtue Honeybee Lady and leader that will cause success, healthy relationships, prosperity, and wealth.
- I will consistently implement a work-life balance scale to avoid burnout.
- Walking in my unapologetic true identity will impact and influence this generation and the next generation of ladies to live and walk in their authentic identity unapologetically.
- As a Virtue Honeybee Lady, I will maintain a healthy balance in life as a whole and get proper rest to steer clear of deficiencies and ineffectiveness.
- I will walk in full grown love as a Virtue Honeybee Lady that expels all kinds of fear.
- My identity is not tied to my accomplishments, validation, or approval from others, but who I am as a lady and leader.

Chapter 3 Restoration
(A Promise of Restoration)

"And that day I will restore the fallen house of David. I will repair its damaged walls. From the ruins, I will rebuild it and restore its former glory." Amos 9:11 (AMP)

If someone ever told you the road to restoration was fun, they lied. To become a candidate for restoration, you first had to be one of the ones that lost it all or enough to feel the loss. If you lose people in your life or things that didn't mean anything to you, you cannot experience restoration. To be restored, is a feeling and a deep seated joy that goes beyond understanding.

When you have been broken, hurt, damaged, abandoned, or rejected, you crave restoration. You want to be made

Chapter 3 Restoration

whole again, and if you find yourself right now needing restoration, please accept my hand. Restoration is a key that opens the door to beautification, blessings, joy, prosperity, peace, good health, hope, success, love, and increases new opportunities in every area of life. Once I embraced and allowed myself to go through the process of rebuilding, I received healing and began the great work of being made whole again. Wholeness and restoration leads to greater success and a better life.

I had to trust this process even when it did not feel good, but I trusted it was going to work out for my good despite what I felt and saw with my natural eyes. Everything works together for our good to those who love God and are called according to His purpose (Romans 8:28 NLT). In my time of transformation, I constantly meditated on a certain verse to help remind me that going through a restoration process old things do re-surface as the healing process takes time to complete.

According to the Webster's 1828 Dictionary, there are four levels to understand the word restoration:
1. To return to a person, as a specific thing which he has lost, or which has been taken from him and unjustly detained. We restore lost or stolen goods to the owner.
2. To replace; to return; as a person or thing to a former place.
3. To bring back.
4. To bring back or recover from lapse, degeneracy, declension or ruin to its former state.

Before I was completely delivered, healed, and restored to whole, my way of thinking, behavior of being overly aggressive and overly assertive, as well as my Ms. Independent mindset needed to be examined. I recalled being sent out on a ministry and business assignment to Indianapolis, IN for a few months in 2017 to 2018. Prior to that time, I had worn the independent woman badge with prestige and honor. At that time I was an 'I' person. I would say things like "I can buy this," "I can do that," "I want to go here not there," "I think this will work better," and "I believe this strategy will yield the best outcome." I could list more examples, but it would be suffice to say, everything started and ended with me, "I" statements.

When I would make those types of "I" statements during the time I was married, my ex-husband would bring it to my attention often. At the time I did not think it was a problem, but after the divorce it was revealed. Those statements I said and many women say are said with sassiness, self-confidence, self-centeredness, and egotistical speech and behavior. I am just being transparent and honest.

Hearing the story from the guy I spoke about at the end of Chapter 2, triggered an old memory and familiar problem I had. The same attitude she has and I hear when women say *"I do not need a man I can buy anything a man would buy for me for myself"*. What good is a man to me?" When I looked back at the comments I made and heard, they were either from a bruised place in my heart or pride due to my status and achievements.

There are elements of over compensation a independent woman must have to mask her true desires to have someone be there with her. Women want to be protected but after realizing someone might not be there, they learn to be there for themselves. Some of these women come

Chapter 3 Restoration

from homes with no positive male figures, fathers, or men that stick around. Being raised in this environment helps shape your ideas on men.

To protect her heart and to provide some degree of comfort, the independent woman will often relish in her accomplishments and earn more money. I can honestly admit I was this type of independent woman and I was flat out broken in that area. I did not know how bad it was until I lost my husband, my children grew distant, and my accomplishments didn't hold the same value in my heart anymore. I was no longer comfortable being broken and masking my pain or disappointment.

Are you at a point in your life where you are just tired of pretending? Now, you are tired of acting like you have it all together because people are scared of you and do what you say. You know in some ways you are being tolerated more than loved, and now for some reason it is no longer good enough. I hit that bottom, but the financial troubles that strained me made it even more challenging to ignore.

Little did I know this new assignment of ministry and business in the marketplace was going to break and destroy the "prestige badge" of being an independent woman. As a woman that likes being in control, I was put in a situation whereby I had to release control by surrendering and trusting the process during this time of my life. Being commissioned to return back to Indianapolis in December 2017 after two years of leaving when my divorce finalized was a challenge in itself.

Arriving in Indianapolis, I didn't have a confirmed job, housing, or clear direction beyond having a strong conviction in my heart. I took a leap of faith and quickly secured housing and a job even during the mist of huge layoffs from the company I was recently employed before leaving Ohio. It was only God's grace which got me through that moment and I started to release that controlling nature I had. I never understood faith like I learned it in those moments. As long as I could cling to my efforts, I could never see my weaknesses.

Can you see a parallel in your attitude and behavior? Are you at a point where you are ready to take a leap of faith to change your life? Faith works and change can make room for restoration. I had to drop the overly aggressive nature if I wanted healthy relationships and the better me to emerge as a mom, a leader, and one day future wife.

This was the starting point of me learning to become more balanced in my view and understanding of an independent woman. Learning to be interdependent in preparation for a future marriage was not my primary focus but a byproduct of being committed to my growth venture. Some of the characteristics of being a balanced Virtue Honey Bee Lady or balanced independent woman include: managing my life effortlessly, taking responsibility for my own happiness, being comfortable in my own skin, embracing change, being financially stable, expecting self-respect and making it a priority, lastly being up for a challenge.

I did not only get the good side of my venture, I also became familiar with the bad and the ugly. Being out of balance as an independent woman I quickly learned included struggling with asking for help even if needed because I feared depending on others. I had to reach

Chapter 3 Restoration

a point to be willing to reverse a childhood belief that I don't have to be an overachiever or only depend on myself. I can become interdependent and all will be well. I hated being perceived as weak, I only wanted to be seen as strong and confident. But always strong can send a misleading message that you do not need anyone's help; that would be false.

I wanted to be in the driver seat making all the decisions and carrying the load. I was familiar with earning my keep, I did not fully understand grace. As I learned to let go of those ways that were hindering me, the better version of me was on display personally and professionally. While in Indianapolis I became responsible for managing and leading the five hospital locations where I was employed in their traveling nurse division and I was a part of the leadership strategy team. Elevation, promotion, increase, and recognition happened in a short few months of me being in that position. I believe the success occurred because I surrendered by letting go of the old unfruitful ways in exchange for fruitful and long lasting success which opened the door for influence and impact.

When restoration begins changes occur in every area of your life. If you are going through this process don't give up on the fight. Do not stop your venture to change. I was returning to my original design before I was influenced by society, movements, sexism, cultural norms, my upbringing, and my view and understanding of life. Learning to have proper balance and the right understanding has been life-changing for me. Subsequently I began to inherit a better and more correct perspective. Various situations occurred and helped push me in the direction of letting go at the time I was unaware. I discovered myself in a profound, unique, brave, purposeful way. The tough girl exterior was shedding away and I was beginning to become more balanced, soft and savvy.

Softness was being restored to me and the honey was being released. I let go of control and let honey enter into the walls of my mind and heart. It was like a huge weight had left my shoulders. As ladies we are designed to be soft, sweet, and gentle as well as bold, fearless, driven, resilient, resourceful, and resolute. No longer do we have to be one over the other, we can and should be both sides of the equation so we can be balanced as a Virtue Honey Bee Lady. Those few months in Indianapolis I allowed myself to be repaired unashamed, to be rebuilt in the proper way to avoid self-sabotaging behavior.

There awaits on the other side of this venture a future that is counting on the present me to make the right decisions. By the time I left Indianapolis I was fully restored in the area I once lacked. As you obtain your equilibrium in being both soft and savvy, having self-control, and being willing to re-adjust, life will get better no matter where your current condition is today. The recent global pandemic made it clear. No one is in complete control, however, we can control our decisions, response, speech, tone, and behavior.

Loyalty

IF you could gather your closest friends to ask them one question, "Are you a loyal person?" What would they say? One of the things I knew about myself growing up and even as an adult, I am a loyal person to the best of my abilities. Being loyal has its benefits and it has

Chapter 3 Restoration

its drawbacks. The benefits include being a faithful person, maintaining confidence, being supportive, honest, dependable, reliable, and consistent in regard to another person's project.

In addition, loyal people strengthen their relationships with others because the relationship fosters an environment of honesty and forthcomingness when they see you are a loyal person. Trust and closeness grows deeper and liberation to be oneself is established in the fabric of building relationships. On the other hand, one of the biggest drawbacks to being loyal is when you remain faithful to toxic or unhealthy relationships.

"Toxic," a common saying we all hear thrown around but at times we may not be clear as to what it means. A toxic relationship can start off healthy and appear with all the normal signs, but at some point the relationship no longer serves in your best interest. If a loyal person is not careful, another person or people could use their commitment to manipulate them to stay in a relationship that is not going anywhere, or do something they may not want to do out of loyalty.

This was me. I was loyal to a fault, even in toxic relationships because I had this inner drive within me that everything I am attached to must succeed and it includes relationships I do not want to fail. I found myself at times more loyal to people who were not as supportive or loyal to me in return. If you have lived, you must have discovered people who are not as supportive for you as you have been for them. If you are on this end of the spectrum it can hurt your heart and shape your future.

On the road to wholeness and restoration, the wisdom I learned after hitting my head on the wall for several years was to set clear boundaries. Effectively communicating clear boundaries and expectations for the relationship and honoring what was established and agreed upon by all parties involved will help loyal ladies remain balanced and avoid heartache, disappointment, or bitterness and resentment. If imbalance occurs and the boundary line gets re-adjusted or moved completely out of the way to accommodate loyalty to the other person or people, the same loyal ladies may become an over aggressive woman who will put demands on the next relationship whether it be in business, leadership, friendship, career, or romantic relationships.

The problem was not with them but within me in the grand scheme of things. People can only do as much as you allow. After all these life lessons in the school of hard knock life, the wisdom, knowledge, and understanding I gained was life changing that helped me set up my life for success in every area of life including my household. If you are a loyal person to a fault with no healthy boundaries in place, I would encourage you to set clear boundaries, expectations, and honor them.

Also, I want to share a word of caution, do not fear your reputation or how others will perceive you. The reality is the boundary lines put in place is an act of loving and respecting yourself. In return others will respect and honor your standard if they truly love you. Disappointment is avoided and restoration becomes your portion along with receiving love and refreshment as you welcome the release of honey in your life. During the time of restoration the soul (mind, will, & emotions), finances, relationships,

Chapter 3 Restoration

family, health, career, marriage and everything connected to you will have a high probability of being restored back to its original state or condition for the better. This condition can predate your existence and understanding. Restoration in the soul in particular enables you to make wise decisions, clears your thoughts, and empowers you to lead effectively and efficiently.

Creativity & Innovation

Creativity and Innovation was another area I experienced restoration from being as I was to becoming beautified as a Virtue Honey Bee Lady. Creativity is defined as the use of imagination or creating new original ideas. I did not realize when I was overly aggressive and a bit up tight it was limiting creativity and innovation from flowing at a higher level through me. Although creativity was within me and I moved in creative things and strategies, I had limitations that affected me. I wanted to be in control, there was lack of flexibility, at times I was narrow minded, and I operated often out of fear.

Inflexibility and desiring to be in control, dominate, or over assert yourself, will strangle creativity or imagination. Innovative ideas will leave you and give you no place to grow and flow freely. How I overcame and experienced growth in the area of creativity and innovation, I learned to become more open minded, eliminating the demand to be in control; and at the same time removing my inflexibility. Giving up fear and control in exchange for freedom and increasing creative ideas seems like a good trade to me. According to the Lutherone Business Series on "The Five Biggest Creativity Killers At Work", the first originality killer is fear. "Fear of being laughed at or criticized by others, fear of making a mistake, fear of being different".

It is easy to play it safe, but it takes courage to break from the norm and dare to be a creative and innovative difference maker not just in business, the church, career, family but in every area of your life. The second area mentioned was tight delivery, the productivity killer. Working under tight delivery or deadlines will hinder anyone's creativity juices to flow because of the time restraint given to complete the task. In those moments quantity and results are the focus. The key to fix that type of situation is to have one solution that will produce the desired results.

The third killer mentioned is complacency, the innovation killer. Change is not always received with a welcoming hug. According to the article "Change is always unpleasant at first, people prefer to accept the way it is now, and they are happy with the way it works." Change is not always necessary, but it does help usher in fresh new ideas, perspective, creativity, and innovation. The fourth is specialization, a combination killer. This occurs when someone is a specialist in different disciplines and she combines different ideas and knowledge. In other words she may be viewed as being all over the place.

The key to fix this dilemma, she will need to determine which discipline she wants to bring forth for her specialized creativity. The fifth biggest Creativity Killer is stress, the leading imagination killer. According to the article, Imagination consists of working with images and complex ideas, and feelings. Imagination requires full concentration, peace, and time. You do not get imagina-

Chapter 3 Restoration

tion on demand and under the pressure of a deadline". If you are a leader in your business, organization or company, create an atmosphere for either yourself or your team to increase in creativity. With the space and time creativity will bring ideas to the table.

Another area I received restoration was from writing. Before I began to write this book, I thought I would write a book directed for both men and women to reach a larger audience. Quickly, I learned I was putting limits on myself and it is possible to write a book design for and with women in mind. The area of doubt was removed, my mind and thoughts surrounding becoming an author catering to ladies was restored.I was able to write with freedom, creativity, and no limitation. I understood I could commit to a work plan with great success.

The same is true for ladies in ministry, business, or in the marketplace running a company or a leader of an organization when restoration occurs it reverse stagnation, increase productivity and efficiency, business is booming, recovery of any loss are gained back, fresh ideas and strategies are implemented, financial increase, exponential growth, new clients or customers, low turn-over rate, higher retention of staff, and higher number of maintain clients and customers.

As I mentioned in the previous chapter, when I walked into levels of fear and rejection for the gratification of being perfect I remained limited, but once I received restoration and allowed myself to be restored those areas were no longer a stronghold or barrier in my life. I desired to be free from those dead ends, the lack of hope, and complacent limited growth and acceleration. Once

the decision was made and I did the necessary work, I gained favor, creativity, deeper strategic thinking, and developed a higher level of esteem and confidence.
The first step I had to do and I highly recommend for any person is self examination and evaluation. I am a firm believer that if we are honest with ourselves we have an opportunity to make better decisions to do better either for ourselves or others. Allow yourself to thoughtfully reflect on your life. The challenges that oppose self-examination and evaluation are being too busy, always on the go, and being out of touch with you. In this part of loving and caring for yourself, there may be fear in learning some truths about you but as difficult as they may be at the time, work through it.

Getting help is not bad, and knowing when you need to reach out is critical. I didn't do it all alone and I don't expect you to do that either. I created a course because I know this is hard and if I could do one thing differently, I would have chosen to have more help as I ventured through this process. I want to encourage you to dig deep, but also allow me to walk with you as the going gets tough. Once you dig and go deeper within yourself you become an active participant in your own examination and evaluation to the road of restoration.

Your willingness to not only actively participate, but engage with yourself on a consistent basis will help work your transformation. Everything you need to transform your life you have with accountability, within you as you tap into every fabric of your being, which is your spirit, mind, will, emotions, and physical being. I want to encourage you to come to my monthly meetups or join my weekly check-ins to help you start or continue on your

Chapter 3 Restoration

journey to recovery.

Restore your original design: soft and savvy,. and Scan the QR Code or connect with me on FB at:

Restoration is the key to your personal and professional life. It will cause fruit to bear and increase evident as you become a Virtue Queen Honeybee Lady.

Shantay Adams

Declaration for Restoration

I decree and declare as a Virtue Queen Honeybee Lady,

- I am restored and have returned back to my original state and condition as a virtue queen honeybee lady.
- I am restored in my mind and thoughts as a thought leader due to restoration.
- I am not a creativity killer; I am restored back to creativity and innovation.
- As a result of allowing restoration to occur in my life, I have been restored to increase, greatness, enlargement, beautification, blessings, prosperity, and success is my portion.
- Creative strategies and ideas will flow out of me because I am restored
- My business, enterprises, company, organization, household, family, marriage, ministry, shall blossom and grow exponentially due to restoration.
- I decree and declare uncommon favor, joy, peace, life, strength, and good health will come to me because of restoration.
- Every broken down wall in my life and around my life as a leader will be restored due to restoration.
- There will no longer be imbalance in loyalty, I have healthy boundary lines that I will honor because of

Chapter 3 Restoration

restoration.
- I embrace restoration to be soft and savvy is my portion.

Chapter 4 Tactful

"In the Battle of Existence, Talent is the Punch; Tact is the Clever Footwork" Wilson Mizner
"Step with Care and Great Talent & Remember that Life's A Great Balancing Act" Dr. Seuss

Communication is a skill, and if you were to ever doubt it, you become a believer when you encounter a person lacking communication. Tactfulness is a big key for good communication. I learned to be thoughtful, careful, respectful, considerate, courteous, understanding, and prudent in my interaction and communication with others. In addition, timing and tone are also included with tactfulness which aids the person to have an acute sense to be farsighted, prevent offense, and cultivate positive relationships.

Chapter 4 Tactful

The words we speak have the power to build, heal, encourage, edify, comfort, and bring peace, love, joy, and happiness. On the other hand, our words have the power to tear down, overwhelm, hurt, disappoint, and discourage. I learned over the years it is not often what a person says, but how they say it. The tone is an indicator of the motive and the condition of the heart. Out of the abundance of the heart the mouth speaks. If the heart is wounded to any degree when it is time to operate with tact, timing, and tone there may be some challenges.

When feelings get involved, our words or body language may appear to be more harsh, lack the proper tone, or timing of when or if not to speak is appropriate. Lacking these linking hospitable actions, the resulting effect is no tact. According to Issac Newton, "Tact is the art of making a point without making an enemy. In other words, a tactful virtue honey bee lady is sensitive to the moment, discerning the potential outcomes, and is judicious in her response. She has the capacity to know and understand it is exceedingly better to dwell in a desert land than with a contentious and troublesome woman who aims to make her point rather than preserve peace.

Peace is to live in harmony, quietness of mind, calmness, reconciliation, and freedom from private or public quarrels or disturbance. No one wants to live in agitation, fear, terror, anger, anxiety, with panic attacks, and constant worry if they don't have to in life. In the years of my life when I did not know I was overly aggressive, overbearing, and wanted to control situations and outcomes, I lacked true peace in my life. I was not tactful in my communication and interaction with others on a consistent basis. I did not exercise the appropriate use of timing and tone. The reason being I was proud, haughty, and foolish.

I know it is hard to use these words to describe ourselves because often we feel like the victim. It is very tempting not to paint yourself a saint and everyone else as your enemy. If you could be honest with yourself, would you say you are guilty of bad timing, tone, or being overbearing or nagging? We don't have to be catty to be treated nicely or receive attention. There were several times I simply said what I thought without any prudence and self control.

When I look back over my life and I think things over this did not start when I became an adult, it began with me being mouthy as a child growing up. I was celebrated for being sharp and sassy. It made the boys respect and back up off clowning me because I was a tough girl that was able to do whatever the boys could do and back it up even in my speech. That behavior and mindset traveled with me. However when I enrolled in the school of hard knock life, my attitude was forever changed. I learned to appreciate and know wisdom from above and the fruit of self-control is a needed companion and life partner. The person who guards his mouth and tongue; guards himself from trouble. (Proverbs 21:23). Also like a city that is broken down and without walls (being unprotected) is a man who has no self-control over his spirit and sets himself up for trouble. (Proverbs 25:28).

When we rule our own spirit with the correct use of tact, timing, and tone we become a better person, leader, wife, daughter, friend, and employee. Furthermore, we will produce honey that generates success, abundance, and

Chapter 4 Tactful

greatness considering the environment is ripe and conducive for the impossible to become possible. I mentioned in the previous chapter restoration when that occurs in our life repairs damaged walls and restores us back to our original design and purpose. The walls in my life became damaged due to pride and it began to show itself in my temperament, attitude, and behavior as an independent woman who went after what she wanted without proper balance and the use of worldly wisdom.

What helped restore the damaged wall was true humility. I had to humble myself. True humility destroys and prevents further destruction of your character. Only the humbles are exalted with a healthy balance to maintain the long lasting fruits of greatness, success, influence, and power. The best and only wisdom is from above, human and world wisdom is insufficient, limited, and quickly grows inadequate. Wisdom from above is pure, undefiled, peace-loving, gentle, reasonable, full of compassion, righteousness, and grace.

When you receive and apply the wisdom from above, a long good life, increase, wealth, and success will be attracted to you. In other words, wisdom along with understanding, and knowledge are necessities for every leader. Ladies who are in leadership wear many hats throughout the day, for instance CEO, Business Owner or Leader, Entrepreneur, Government or City Official, Military, Healthcare Leader, World Leader, First Lady, Mother, Wife and the list can go on and on. The key to making the transition smooth between your life's demands is pure wisdom and knowledge.

When you have tact, timing, and tone they are the vehicles in which the wise leader executes her transition with wisdom at the helm. Choice is exceedingly greater than any human effort. Choosing wisdom from above will help you make the right decisions, but the choice will always be yours and the adventure you take can work to your good no matter your choice. Divine wisdom helps us bear all things but it doesn't remove every obstacle.

With wisdom, we are better prepared to select the right people to do business with, and choose the right partner for marriage, or avoid loss or heartache, within your team that may cause a negative domino effect. The opposite is true when one does make the right conscious decision there is a positive domino effect at play. You will notice things will work out for your good and situations fall in pleasant places. 'I have learned that short success is good, but it is far greater to plan and strategize for long lasting success. Those wins shape your future, create your legacy, and build your influence as a leader not only to the people you serve, but also to various cultures and generations.

Influential leaders are driven by the desire to change lives for the better. Being a difference maker for the good of others means serverving by providing insight and information. In essence influential leaders are purpose minded, effective, driven, distinguished, instrumental, and inspiring. Their impact in an organization, community, or within their family is undeniable because their action and insight greatly influence the course of events. As a leader, being and remaining influential is of high importance for long lasting success and great accomplishments. Virtue Queen Honey bee Ladies are influential leaders who use tactfulness to become Influ-

Chapter 4 Tactful

ential leaders.

Becoming and remaining tactful as a leader shows character, integrity, professionalism, maturity and it allows you to preserve relationships and build new ones. As mentioned earlier in this chapter, tactfulness with the right timing and tone demonstrates one's ability to communicate with others utilizing grace, consideration, diplomacy and prudence fosters mutual respect. According to Pauline Ziegler's blog on "Diplomacy and Tact: The Essentials of Leadership In 2023," she defines diplomacy as "the practice of influencing people's decisions and behavior through negotiations, discussion, and preventing the arousal of hostility." In any kind of relationship whether it is intimate, personal with family or friends, colleagues, or business it is important to be sensitive to someone's feelings.

We cannot control how a person will respond, but we can communicate in a loving way. We can respect people's opinions whether right or wrong, and their thoughts on a matter even if we do not agree so that we can better solve problems. This attitude helps increase favorable outcomes for parties for challenging or even stressful conversations. Pauline stated five things are essential for successful tact and diplomacy I do believe are a part of the DNA of a tactful influential leader.

The first is to "Listen attentively to both what is being said and how it is stated." In short, listening for understanding and not to respond is a common practice of any good communicator. You cannot hear someone if you are already thinking of your response when they start talking. "Emotional intelligence is the awareness we have for how we feel and others. If a person effectively communicates with more diplomacy and tact along with timing and tone that person has a higher emotional intelligence IQ.

We know that you can catch more of anything with honey, being polite, than rude with an attitude. Being polite helps bridge the gap for the difference of opinion and cultures. It also builds relationships with strangers for temporary use and benefit. Building relationships is important because rapport, the strength of your connection with someone, will get you referrals, recommendations, and free promotion. With a positive rapport, people will willfully talk you up and present you in a positive light. The opposite is true for negative rapport so guard your representation and experiences with others to work in your favor.

Being assertive, is speaking in a firm tone and confidence level that moves other people to get involved and follow instructions. No one wants to be a doormat and have people walk over them. If people are not respecting your words, thoughts, or instructions, you likely are not assertive enough.

The last is "assertiveness, to influence others to think or behave in a certain way." A healthy balance of assertiveness is sometimes warrant for example, when a team you are leading needs some persuasion to get the job done or for you to negotiate and close a deal. Influential leaders are Virtue Honeybee Ladies understand diplomacy, tact, timing, and tone is an art that takes a certain level of discipline, skills, and continuous practice. In addition, choosing to be prudent and use wise words with appropriate body language are also keys to become or remain

Chapter 4 Tactful

a successful leader. Doing so creates a win-win environment and solutions.

I stated earlier in this chapter that there is not a heavier weight on what a person says rather than how the person says it, but also their body language. Your eyes shifting up to the sky, your hand motioning for dismissal, flipping your hair and turning your head, or turning your back on someone to walk away all have a meaning. You must be aware of what you are saying by words, action, and tone.

If one of these elements is off or constantly used negatively it will pull down the morale of a team, relationships, and the success of you being a quality leader. That was a lesson I learned in marriage and leadership. When I intentionally aligned my non-verbal and verbal communication tactfully and with diplomacy it became a recipe for success in every area of my life.

As I strive continuously to be and remain a Virtue Honeybee Lady, diplomacy is upheld. According to the article, Pauline Ziegler stated "People who practice the art of diplomacy are called diplomats, because they maintain peace and promote cooperation among organizations, and nations." These individuals cultivate an atmosphere where people effectively work together collaboratively, increase productivity, reduce turnover, maintain higher retention of staff, and win over existing or new clients and customers time after time.

If your home or business is in constant conflict with no resolve, you may need to take a second look at being more tactful. It is not that you are saying the wrong things, it may be how you are conveying those problems, or presenting the solutions. Diplomats are not as concerned about being right and showcasing that truth as they are more committed to peace and progress. Learning to not be the center of every solution will help you demonstrate more tact.

Remaining tactful also means being humbled. Humility will allow you to be diplomatic and put the business, marriage, or relationship before your desire to feel acknowledged for being right. I was once told, if you are traveling through a traffic light and your light changes from red to green. You look over and see a car not stopping, do you proceed through the traffic light because it is your turn or allow the other person to go? It is better to be alive than dead right.

This type of character trait is foundational to establishing and building a good name and healthy reputation that has the high probability to bring honor, prestige, and prominent distinction to that leader that separates her from the common leader to the uncommon first class effective leader notoriety. Therefore, it is a must to have and apply in your leadership tool kit to be a solutionist and one who does not only manage conflict but has the expertise to solve them as needed.

As I learn to be effective as a person who understands and embraces my true identity in the world, I took the necessary steps to develop, mature, grow, and become more effective in tact, timing, and tone in both ministry and business as a leader. I am a firm believer that the only person that can stop you from reaching your full potential, purpose, and destiny is you. That is why I spend time in self-reflection and self-examination to be in tune

Chapter 4 Tactful

with myself as a person, a mom, a daughter, a friend, and as a leader. I do this in an effort to see if there are any areas within me that will hinder or sabotage where I am purpose and destined to head in life.

I want you to take a moment and ask yourself the question, where am I headed? Is my attitude, tactfulness, humility, and diplomacy working for me or against me? By being honest, you will know best what you should do next. It would be to work on those troubled areas and find resources to help bridge the gaps. Unmasking, and make a point to make adjustments or remove obstacles completely. I said to myself some time ago, I unapologetically desire the full future that awaits me. Can you say that right now, "I unapologetically desire the full future that awaits me!"

The power you just released into the atmosphere, the honey, will start to bring out beautiful truth. Do understand, idol words do not produce results and change. Your words must be coupled with actions, follow through if you want to obtain this future you envision. You must do your part effectively, diligently, with discipline to receive the inherit promise that has already been written. Take some time and allow yourself to self-reflect and self-examine a person and then as a leader.

As I learn and believe you will also come to agree that doing a self inventory is tremendously beneficial and promotes growth and development as a Influential Virtue Honeybee Lady and Leader. As you follow through on this venture to pick up tools to improve your mindset, you will become a person and leader that is bold, courageous, has grit, and is fearless. Some leaders do not understand the importance nor apply the skills of being tactful during communication, providing feedback on topics, or handling sensitive matters, however, implementing these tactics and diplomacy, will effectively change your life.

According to an American Psychologist Association article, "What are the Benefits of Mindfulness" it states that researchers theorize that mindfulness meditation promotes metacognitive awareness, decreases rumination via disengagement from perseverative cognitive activities, and enhances attentional capacities through gains in working memory. These cognitive gains, in turn, contribute to effective emotion regulation strategies." As a leader in the home or outside the home, mindfulness assists you in forming enhanced listening skills to become more constructive and productive in relationships. Combined with increased focus helps you better connect with others and boost creativity and innovation.

Creativity and innovation was mentioned in the previous chapter Restoration, under the topic what kills creativity. Mindfulness amplifies creativity and innovative ideas and new methods. Tactfulness, diplomacy, and mindfulness help you not to act fast without any filter. Being overly aggressive or assertive, or speaking without any thought to how the other person will receive it is not wise. I shared with you in the second chapter about a woman who went on a first date with a man and she was offended by him wanting to pay for their meal. She responded with aggression because she believes as an independent self-sufficient modern day woman that she can pay her own bills and does not need a man. The woman on the first date was financially stable and accomplished

Chapter 4 Tactful

in her career but she lacked tact, diplomacy, mindfulness, and as a result she was unsuccessful in her personal life in the area of relationships.

Yes it is possible for you to perform and have great success although these areas are lacking in your life. A better question or consideration to make, if I am doing great now, imagine what you can accomplish when you learn how to employ tact and diplomacy? As a leader skipping this lesson is non-negotiable if you don't want to fall on your face or reach a glass ceiling limiting your career or business. As a person that has worked in the human resource industry for over a decade plus, I have heard individuals say they could not work with this leader or that leader and wanted to leave the organization or company because of it. Look for the telltale signs that demonstrate something is lacking and work to implement the changes to keep your staff, develop your business, or sure up your communication for the success of your business, family, or marriage.

Tact is foremost for ladies in leadership or if you are a leader in hopes of maintaining healthy relationships or starting new relationships personally or professionally. If I can be of help, I am here to walk you through this phase and get a plan implemented to teach you the skills you need to grow and overcome some long overdue problems. Let's get to work!

Shantay Adams

Declaration for Tactful

I decree and declare as a Virtue Queen Honeybee Lady,

- I am tactful.
- I am an influential tactful leader that provides first class service and leadership.
- I will use prudence and wisdom from above in my actions and speech because I understand the art of tactfulness and diplomacy.
- I will aim to preserve peace and be tactful in my response and approaches with the right timing and tone.
- I will be a successful leader in every area that I am called to lead or co-lead and the fruit will be evident.
- As an influential leader, my walls are strong and healthy because I walk in true humility and willingness to serve others.
- My name will go before me in rooms I have not yet entered because I am a Virtue Queen Honeybee that has a good name and reputation as one who is tactful, uses mindfulness and diplomacy as a leader.
- I have a healthy emotional intelligence IQ.

Chapter 4 Tactful

Chapter 5 Unstoppable
"Confidence is key - once you have that, you are unstoppable." Timothy Weah
"Believe in yourself and you will be unstoppable." Emily Guay

Do you feel you are unstoppable or that your life is filled with stops. Your dreams are stopped. Your plans for marriage are stopped! Your plans for leadership are stopped! If you are married or dating the love that used to be there has stopped! Your well appears to be running dry and you have had to stop what you are doing and ask the question, why?

Why is my life in hold, or why have I stopped progressing? Sometimes the lack of progress is not because things are not happening but because something has

Chapter 5 Unstoppable

shifted within us. Not all shifts are toward the good. When doubt creeps in, it is sent to come for your confidence, hope, and future. Don't allow the lack of confidence to make you shy away from what is yours. Go for it!

When I learned and began to walk in the power of *being,* it increased my confidence and brought my self esteem to another level. Sometimes we need to check ourselves to see where we place on the confidence and esteem spectrum. When I reached the phase of being unstoppable in a healthy way, becoming an unstoppable Virtue Queen Honey Bee Lady, it was a game changer for my personal and professional life.

This confidence wasn't based on attitude or reaching for a mask to hide behind, it was earned. In the last chapter, I mentioned the only person that can stop you from reaching your goals and excelling in our predetermined purpose and destiny is you. Yes, there are life situations and circumstances that will happen that will block or attempt to stop or slow you down. However, we are more than conquerors, we have the grace and ability to work to overcome any obstacle while we have breath. In the moments and times we feel at our weakest, we must press harder by leaning on our source, practicing what we have learned, enduring the friction that comes, and choose to persevere becoming laser-focused on succeeding.

You will not get a lot of wins focusing on your losses. You can learn from your losses but don't let them define you. Instead become resilient and resolute. In 2022 I watched a movie titled "90 Minutes in Heaven" that made the big screen in 2015. In an attempt to do a quick overview of the true story it was based on this young minister named Don Piper, his calling and purpose in ministry, and his family. Don Piper was traveling alone back home from a ministry conference assignment on January 18, 1989 and there was a downpour of heavy rain.

The rain made the visibility challenging as he drove down the street. While he was driving down the road he ended up in the wrong lane, and slammed into a semi truck head on. Piper was pronounced dead by the first rescue worker and three sets of EMTs after. The body of Piper laid under a tarp for 90 minutes. Doing that time he went to heaven but he returned back to earth. A witness that was on the scene during the time of the accident believed in the power of prayer and he had a strong desire to pray.

Dick Onarecker, a pastor as well, prayed and miraculously a few moments later, Piper's heart started to beat again. The recovery road ahead for Piper and his family was going to be one that required endurance and perseverance. When Don Piper made the decision to fight for his life, despite doctors not expecting him to live even after arriving at the hospital. Don overcame severe injuries, depression, sadness, hurt, and grief from being separated from his old life. He was not used to being cared for primarily because he was usually the caregiver and provider in the past.

As he overcame every setback and challenges along with his wife, they both came out on top; together they were unstoppable. As Piper was recovering and able to go outside the home, doors began to open for him to testify

Chapter 5 Unstoppable

and share his story. The more strength that came to Don Piper's mind and body he and his family began to experience restoration that was evident, success was amplified, and their darkest time became a message and a movie to encourage and inspire others to not give up but to have faith and marry it with perseverance. They became better versions of themselves and Don Piper discovered the deepness of his calling and purpose for his life.

This movie inspired me. I had to mention it within this book particularly for this chapter. It serves as a reminder that when life throws a curveball, endure, persevere, and do not throw in the towel. Similar to the Piper's when we get to the other side of adversity life does get sweeter like honey. After my divorce I had to learn how to function and operate as a single mom. I must admit it was a challenge for me for a period of time.

Suddenly, there was no partner to help carry the weight and responsibilities in the home. The reality of the situation forced me to grow up in a way I did not see coming. The emotions and challenges I was dealing with eventually permeated in the household and my children felt some of my struggle. Although I put on a brave face, I still had moments where it was hard. Prior to the divorce, financially we were not where we wanted to be, but we did okay, and were not lacking. Post divorce I began to experience some financial struggles and I had to re-budget as a single mom.

All the bills were on me, yes, I was receiving help from my ex-husband, but I quickly learned a two income household is always better than one. I also learned to be both the father and the mother at times and it pushed me to become more aggressive, because I was raising two sons along with my daughter and her daughter, my granddaughter. Once I made the decision to pick up the pieces and push forward, life got a little easier. The fighter inside of me believed I was unstoppable and the best had not yet to come in my life. Adapting the attitude of "I can do this" along with a winning mindset despite the setbacks and challenges I had to keep.

As my attitude got increasingly better and I had the proper perspective of life as a whole, things began to shift in my favor. Over time I became stronger, more confident, and unstoppable. This spirit filled energy spilled over into my professional life. Realizing and understanding the magnitude of being the only breadwinner in the home, it was not an option. My children depended on me, they looked up to me as a role model, and I believe in setting a good example publicly and privately to this present day for them. Recently, my oldest son was interviewing for a summer camp counselor position and the interviewer asked him "Who does he consider to be his role model and why?"

I was not home during their zoom call, but my youngest was home with his brother and he called during the interview and shared with me my son's response. He said, "My mom because when she sets her mind to do something she gets it done." That touched my heart and all those years of overcoming life's different challenges my son saw the effort, excellency, drive, discipline, and diligence to provide for our household. Learning to keep a good attitude and remaining calm under pressure to the best of my abilities, I believe has and is teaching all my children to remain calm in life's storm.

Chapter 5 Unstoppable

Keep a good attitude because it brings peace. Our household was one of peace because I learned I set the tone of the house. If your house is in chaos, check yourself and identify if you are starting the fire. Is your house a reflection of your character, wants, and desires? Living and walking in a lifestyle of peace yields great blessing, prosperity, increase, success, and peace with others. If you do not have this, let's talk more about how you can obtain it the same as I did.

It took a few years to consistently value peace and not feel like I had to prove my point at every chance. I was that person who was used to fighting for my position from childhood to adulthood. I am familiar and very comfortable with arguing my point to the wheels falling off, figuratively speaking of course. As I grew and matured with deeper truth and understanding, I became protective of my peace whether at home, in the office, or out publicly.

Peace in the heart and mind leads to better decisions being made as a leader, in your career path, business dealings, financial decisions, or investment and really every part of your life. The person with peace is single minded not double-minded. When a person is not operating from a place of peace, a sign is that the person is extremely indecisive. Once the person's mind is made up it is changed like the blowing of the wind. Another sign of a lack of peace and double mindedness occurs when the person is often found in arguments or heated exchanges. This person probably lacks peace at home, in the neighborhood, or in her career, and the biggest reason being she freely gives her peace away.

Shantay Adams

We may think we are not contributing to our lack of peace but our decisions would point to otherwise. If you find that you cannot keep a sound mind, you are in a battle for your peace. You have to allow yourself to make decisions and trust yourself. In an effort to make a point or get the final word, we can step outside of our ideal character. Let's face it, we are not perfect and everyone starts from somewhere. Don't let anyone bring you back to a point you no longer belong. The lack of peace, confidence, endurance, perseverance, not able to overcome obstacles, and double-mindedness are strong hindrances to becoming unstoppable as a leader. Instead, the woman in leadership will either become stuck or it will take her longer to achieve her goals and fulfill her purpose due to self-limitation.

Removing most of your hindrances will make you an unstoppable Virtue Queen Honey Bee Lady is bold, courageous, resolute, full of peace, and a single-minded warrior. Not a warrior that has to be overly aggressive, argumentative, or dominating to lead or rise to the top. A warrior, however, is guided by her inner defined voice that leads her gently with wisdom and understanding.

This amazing woman is ready to take over the world, full of energy and excitement. She is laser-focused to accomplish her goals and as Vince Lombardi famously said, "Winners never quit and quitters never win." What separates winners from quitters is a *decision* to remain unstoppable. Recently I was presented with a business trip to a conference in Atlanta for Coaches, Consultants, and Speakers, and Thought Leaders. I wanted to attend this event and I knew it would be beneficial and a blessing to me, but at that time there were circumstances in

Chapter 5 Unstoppable

my life I perceived were limiting me and my children. Life never stops does it?

Like me, I am sure you have living expenses, relationship situations, and may even be in the throes of moving physically, emotionally, or spiritually in a different direction. In my mind the timing did not seem right to go on this trip. However things changed when I was listening to the audible book of T. Harv Eker, "Secrets of the Millionaire Mind; Mastering the Inner Game of Wealth." He asked the question, "Will you be a person that will be stopped or a person that won't be stopped."

When I heard that statement I was laying on my bed. Keep in mind, I have listened to this book more than once, but on that particular day, I sprung up so fast and decided I am going to go to Atlanta. I knew in my heart that the statement through T. Harv Eker used to push me to make a decision and shift my mindset to press through the obstacles and circumstances that wanted to block me. These obstacles desire to stop you from receiving the connections, amazing business breakthroughs, information, greater insight, counsel, and strategies available in the room. If you are a spiritual person, you would say the devil tried to hold you back, but honestly, you are.

When I sprung up from my bed I said to myself, I choose to be a person who won't be stopped because of the grace, power, and ability of the greater that is inside of me. Eker empowered me to encourage other ladies who were invited to this trip and experiencing some personal and private obstacles to press and come also. Sometimes we need to be encouraged by a helping voice not that we can't do it ourselves, but because people were created to live in community. I needed a community of believers, visionaries, and go getters around me.

The response from the ladies was amazing and I believe there were some who planned not to go but changed their minds and came to Atlanta. We don't always know how our voice will help others move forward, but give what you can when you can. I was grateful to have been blessed with encouragement and to turn around and bless others. That brought my heart great joy and planted a seed in me to keep going! If I had not gone to Atlanta, I would not have learned and gained wisdom for the things that were on the horizon for my life.

It is not about knowing every step but the next best step that gets you going in the right direction. As planners, we want to know all the details and element the chance for error. The truth, some things take faith and a leap to get it going. Also, if I had not gone I would not have gotten a chance to be in the same room as Dr. Sonja Stribling and sit under her teaching and coaching.

At the conference I got an opportunity to be imparted with some wise nuggets from Les Brown who surprised all of us including the host. Each day was phenomenal and it was an impactful and transformative trip. It was during this event I also got the opportunity to meet my self publisher, KLE Publishing. Dr. Krystal Lee what it was in her heart to connect with me further after the trip and immediately when we got back from Atlanta things were unstoppable. Doors were being pushed open wide and to my surprise, greater things kept coming way beyond what I thought lying on my bed that day.

Chapter 5 Unstoppable

Honestly speaking, I am so grateful and humbled by it all. In that moment sitting on my bed making the decision to remain unstoppable and investing in myself ultimately for a better life for my children, grandchildren, was life-changing. There is a song by McFadden and Whitehead titled, "Ain't No Stopping Us Now" and that song is my mentality at this stage of my life and beyond. There is a part that says,

If you felt we've been held down before
I know you'll refuse to be held down anymore!
Don't you let nothing, nothing
Stand in your way!
I want ya'll to listen, listen
To every word I say, every word I say!
Ain't No Stoppin Us Now!
We're on the move!
Ain't No Stoppin Us Now!

As I write some of the lyrics it is empowering and encouraging me even now to keep going. I have a mentality to not let obstacles hold me back and I hope the same for you is developing if it is not yet present. Continue to be a leader who will rise to the occasion and defeat every roadblock that wants to stand in your way. Remember, you are more than a conqueror, you are an overcomer.

Once a leader becomes unstoppable, she has the ability to have greater impact, influence, and will be an inspiration for other ladies. According to Kontact Consulting, " 8 Secrets to Becoming an Unstoppable Leader and Achieving Success," they are as follows:

- ***Define your vision***

- *Develop clear communication*
- *Cultivate a strong work ethic,*
- *Creativity and innovation*
- *Embrace failure*
- *Practice continuous personal growth*
- *Build a strong team*
- *Lead by example.*

Nothing can be done without first defining your vision which is where you want to go. Defining your vision is paramount for any leader or person for the reason being one has to see it before they can materialize it in the natural world. Another reason it is essential to have a vision is to establish the why for motivation. According to Kontact Consulting, "Without a clear understanding of what you want to achieve and why it's impossible to complete the journey to becoming an unstoppable leader."

I couldn't agree more, but do you agree? Can you see yourself where you want to go? Can you see beyond your current condition and predicament? In embracing your failures, you are able to see where you are and determine how best to go where you desire. Denial is how you stay stagnant. Don't beat yourself up if you feel you have failed, look at what contributed to it, then make changes. According to the article, "Most successful leaders, entrepreneurs, and innovators understand this, and they embrace failure as an opportunity to learn and grow, and improve. We become more resilient and adaptable, better able to handle challenges, setbacks, and learn to approach obstacles as opportunities, and use failure as fuel to push us forward."

Chapter 5 Unstoppable

Good leaders, the same as entrepreneurs and business owners, are great problem solvers. Over the years in my personal life I have learned to look at failure as a time to learn lessons and apply the wisdom, knowledge, and understanding of what to do better if there should be a next time. It took me many years to truly embrace failure as a good thing and see it for something more than disappointment. When I first launched the business I was graced to start, it was not a great success out the gate buta failure. Looking at it positively, it was a very slow start and it quickly went into the negative digits.

The business did not take off like I hoped and envisioned. Although there were some things I got to do under the business that was a success, I needed a team to help the vision come to pass. I learned the importance and value of having an excellent team that desires to see the vision come to life and flourish. An unstoppable influential virtue honeybee leader has a team and is not in the hive doing everything on her lonesome. She has a calling on her life to lead, but not in a exploitive way, but as such to help those around her. She reaches out and effectively impacts this world without compromising personal values, morals, or integrity.

Did you know that leading with integrity and empathy are the mainsprings for effective leadership? Developing and increasing in those mainsprings builds trust and confidence among followers who will in return be committed to the leader. In addition, it builds trust with customers and clients. I have learned over the years to maintain a daily walk in integrity for both my personal and professional life. I value being a woman of my word and keeping things confidential that are shared with me.

Of course, providing timely and truthful communication takes courage because we may have to say something someone doesn't want to hear.

Don't get discouraged to compromise but work out of love and compassion. Strong moral principles are your ability to be aware and understand people's thoughts and feelings while simultaneously providing appropriate response and support even during hard conversation will distinguish you as a leader. The unstoppable leader in leadership and business practice will create a positive reputation, healthy environment, cultivate excellent relationships, and share a positive culture.

In the end, the key to becoming, mastering, and maintaining an unstoppable leader's mindset starts with a decision to refuse to quit and remain resolute and resilient. Situations and circumstances will arise sometimes that are out of our control, but do not let them define you, stop you, or cause you to throw in the towel in those moments. You have to press in harder, because this is the pressure needed to make you an unstoppable influential Virtue Honey Bee Lady. No one becomes strong by never being challenged, the same as you never pass if you won't take the test.

Next, you have to make a shift in your mindset to remain single-minded, despite the failures that may occur, and not let them stop you from fulfilling your vision and purpose. Lastly, every unstoppable leader must know and understand their "why" in order to overcome adversities, setbacks, and challenges. Adopting the mindset and encouraging yourself with the *"I can" and "I will overcome"* attitude will help you become an unstoppable leader.

Chapter 5 Unstoppable

This inner self talk will build up your inner confidence to know if you graciously did it before, you can do it again. Remain confident with humility even when others do not see nor understand the vision you have. Keep going forward and celebrate each accomplishment you have great or small. As a Virtue Queen Honeybee Lady, recognizing the power and life flowing within you helps you to overcome any obstacle faced. You will not be stopped, but shall conquer all gracefully, and have great success.

Shantay Adams

Declaration for Unstoppable

I decree and declare as a Virtue Queen Honeybee Lady,

- I will walk as an unstoppable influential Virtue Honey bee Lady.
- I will remain courageous, fearless, bold, and audacious as an unstoppable leader in my personal and professional life.
- I will remain resilient and resolute as an unstoppable leader who refuses to quit.
- I will lead with integrity and empathy to help ensure great success.
- I will honor the vision given to me along with my "why" and go forth unstoppably.
- I will continue to adopt the "*I can*" and *"I will overcome"* attitude in my personal and professional life.
- I will flourish as an unstoppable influential leader who will effectively impact this world.
- I will do phenomenal things as a leader in leadership as I remain unstoppable.

Chapter 5 Unstoppable

Chapter 6 Excellence

"Excellence is giving your outstanding effort to do right with the understanding perfectionism is not the goal nor is it achievable." Shantay Adams

Have you ever been nitpicked to death? Everything you do, someone is over your shoulders making noises or telling you what to and not to do. The spirit of perfectionism has caused many of us to lose sleep and great relationships. Can you relate to knowing people like this? How did they make you feel?

In chapter one I spoke about the years I aimed for perfection rather than excellence. Honestly, I was the person who would micromanage people to ensure results. I was that way in both my personal and professional life, everything had to be perfect in my eyesight. If I had to stay up all night to get a particular project done–my way, I would because at that time in my life, I was afraid of failure. Desiring for people to only see the best side of me, and not my vulnerability, flaws or shortcomings, I overcompensated in the worst way.

To add to that point, there is nothing wrong with any person striving to be their best or wanting that for their business. We all should aim to be the best version of ourselves and better than who we were the previous day or years ago. According to Good therapy.org, "Perfectionism is often defined as the need to be or appear to be perfect, or even to believe that it's possible to achieve." I did have a need in my mind to be an overachiever and ambitious with no healthy boundaries starting from my childhood into adulthood. Perfectionism and even becoming overly aggressive in nature was rooted in the fear of failure, fear of rejection, and pride.

That same fear and pride would keep me up late and motivated me to keep going when I really needed rest or a new perspective. Have you ever went headstrong in the wrong way? Did you have regrets or thought to do things differently next time? How is that going? Sometimes we can have good intentions but still fall short of making the necessary changes in our lives. Don't fall short of your commitment to change your life by not following through with your goal to do something different.

There was a standard in my mind and I had to obtain that standard with little or no mistakes. I did not have grace for myself to fall short of my vision either. Even if others saw what I was doing or working on was good enough, if it did not meet my standards it was rubbish. Do you throw your writings, drawings, dreams, or ideas in the trash because they don't meet your standards?

I questioned myself on why I had such a powerful pull to perfectionism. I realized it wasn't just for one reason but multiple that I had adapted this deep seated mindset. One of the things that fueled that symptom of perfectionism was the fact I was highly competitive. I did not compete nor compare myself with others as much as I set a demand on myself to produce flawless output. I wanted to be efficient and feel valuable beyond question.

I was results driven and that in a holistic way is very helpful, but out of balance, can ruin your life. During those years of my life if I made a mistake at school, work, or did not attain the results I had planned, I would take it extremely hard and my attitude would reflect. I would become in rage blowing smoke and fire everywhere I turned because I was emotionally unstable. That attitude didn't turn off at work or at school, but came home with me and everyone in the house would feel the effect.

The reason for the poor attitude was my lack of emotional maturity, I didn't know how to respond to failure. I saw failure as a disease, a cancer that had to be dealt with aggressively to save the whole. The perfectionist overachiever's behavior and mindset was also fueled by me wanting to be admired by others. I wanted to be liked and I loved the attention of being recognized for my good grades, work ethic, achievements and accomplishments both personally and professionally.

Who doesn't want to be complemented for well behaved

Chapter 6 Excellence

children, having a good marriage, and working her dream job and excelling doing it? My need didn't seem like it was coming from a bad place, and it wasn't. It was my follow through and heart towards achieving the goal that soured the taste of success. This unhealthy behavior carried on into my marriage, and it was not until I was divorced that I was ready to receive some truth about me.

If I was open to feedback, who's to say if my marriage would have turned out differently, but I can say I would have been different. If your marriage is on the rocks and you have a heart and mind to preserve it, I encourage you to do the work for you. It is never someone else's problem for how you act but yours. I thought someone else's shortcomings could justify my attitude and response. The truth, I learned it does not.

Perfectionism was and is extremely exhausting, it is never obtained and a perfectionist person will always find fault. No matter how hard I worked, or someone worked to please me, I could nitpick to find a problem for me to solve. The obvious reason that occurs is because their expectations are too high, unrealistic, and they push their fear on others. If you want to be admired, you don't want anyone to ruin that image; that includes your children and spouse.

According to Good Therapy.org, "Self-critical perfectionism is more prone to becoming intimidated by the goals they set for themselves rather than feeling motivated." In other words, the perfectionist suffers a lot from self-condemnation, being overly critical of themselves or others, being overly aggressive, overly ambitious, easily becoming frustrated and stressed out. The fear of failure is present and the thought of losing control is their worst nightmare. I know all these things to be true because I was her.

Perfectionism is not the big bad wolf, however, it did push me to have a high work ethic, but at a hefty cost. There are some professions where maximum precision is required and that could lead to life or death. Do you want a doctor who is always late or procrastinating doing your surgery? Would you value their opinion if they were not perceived to be perfect and without fault? Is that not our expectation of doctors and high performing professionals including political figures, they have to be perfect?

When I began the adventure of becoming free from the bondage of perfectionism and its roots, I had to get comfortable with having less control. I had to learn that mistakes are not that bad and they are a part of life. Mistakes are not failure, I quickly learned that lesson, and began to apply the wisdom gained to move forward. As I was breaking free of perfectionism I began to learn divine excellence.

I no longer had to be admired by others in order to feel accomplished. Excellence to me is giving outstanding effort by doing the right thing with the understanding perfectionism is not the goal nor is it achievable. Aiming for excellence over perfectionism caused a lot of unnecessary weight to fall off of me, figuratively. Over the years as I learned, grew, and evolved as a person, excellence became a traveling companion to this present day.

Knowing I put my best foot forward in the spirit of excellence brought incredible peace to me and perhaps

Chapter 6 Excellence

those around me during that time of my life. As deeper truth, knowledge, and understanding came to me, and I learned that excellence is a moral virtue. Compelled by the information received, I had a strong desire in my heart and mind to do everything intentionally with excellence.

During that transformation and my intentional daily walk personally and professionally, I implemented daily decrees and declarations of excellence over my life. Walking in excellence was the honey I needed to become a Virtue Honeybee Lady in life and leadership. Honey is the sweet ingredient that helps create and establish balance; assisting me with identifying areas of continuous improvement for the better. According to Terri Kozlowski article, "Four Aspects of Excellence That You Can Achieve," she stated, "By developing habits of excellence, we achieve influence and stand out from the pack. By cultivating a culture of greatness, we attract new supporters and win the loyalty of long-standing associates."

Creating a culture of greatness and excellency cannot be underrated nor short change because it is one of the key ingredients to success. This type of culture demonstrates consistency and places a high commitment level starting with the leader, then to the team to operate in excellence. Leading by example is another key ingredient to establishing a culture of greatness and excellence. I am a leader who leads by example first in my household and then the marketplace. I have shown my children if I do not do it first and show them the correct way, how can I expect that from them.

The same is true for leadership in the marketplace. I am

a hands-on leader who understands trust, consistency, and relationship building if done right are factors that will determine the success and longevity of the leader's business, organization, or company. In the article, Kozlwski pointed out the connection between excellence and competence. She stated, "To gain a reputation for quality means delivering great results every time and those who repeatedly demonstrate competence gain credibility." Competence is the ability to do something efficiently with success and excellence.

Competence is needed to do anything but especially for a leader. Both excellence and competence are needed in a leaders tool kit along with continuous improvement, learning, developing, and growing. As a leader I often say humbly I am a lifetime learner even if I am asked to facilitate or teach on a subject, my heart is open to learn more. Leaders of excellence and competency are rewarded with loyalty and support and that is a win for everyone. The effects of an inferior and incompetent leader cause financial loss for both the leader and the organization or company for where they are employed.

This leader will experience a decline in performance, low morale, turn over increases, and additional costs are incurred to hire. A leader with a grip on excellence and competence understands the two doesn't equal perfectionism but limiting the risk of mistakes that will inevitably happen. Insurance exists because it takes one time to make a life altering mistake. No one goes out saying I want to get into an accident, but they happen everyday and often. I can understand employees who leave companies because they want to establish a culture norm of continuous improvement, development, and training. Of

Chapter 6 Excellence

incompetent leadership and unrealistic expectations.

What I have discovered to be of great benefit and I implemented in my personal and professional life is the honey of self-discipline. Self-discipline has helped me be balanced in my daily life with health and exercise, also in my commitment to excellence. As I have already mentioned in this chapter, I was once a person that strived for perfection in an unhealthy way. Therefore by grace, I had to re-train my mind, speech, behavior, and discipline myself so I would not revert back to old habits that did not produce long lasting fruits of success. The discipline helped me further respond to tasks, goals, projects, or plans in a healthy, excellent way until it became second nature embedded in my subscious. I was conditioning myself.

Similar to a basketball player who is developing his or her skills and body to perform on a high level, he or she must become disciplined in workouts and training. The more disciplined and committed they are with developing their body and skills, the more condition they will become and it will show up on the basketball court. How disciplined have you been with your attitude, patience, need to be perfect, and ability to allow others–including yourself to make mistakes?

Practice makes it permanent. Self-discipline is a power within a Virtue Honeybee leader that will propel her to persevere even when she may want to give up. In addition, self discipline will help her as a leader to avoid the temptation to become overly aggressive, but rather walk in a spirit of excellence, self-control, motivation, persistence, and goal orientation. An overly aggressive woman or leader can come off too strong, inflexible, bossy, impatient, too independent, critical of others, quick tempered, is a workaholic, and tends to make decisions for others because of their take charge nature. Unknowingly she intrudes into others' space and they have a hard time admitting they were wrong or made a mistake. Most leaders are widely recognized as being assertive but that does not mean aggressive.

There is a thin line between assertive leadership and aggressive leadership and I learn honey and self discipline are the ingredients in the middle that has helped me not cross the line as a lady leader. I am softy but savvy and I have a soft, balanced, and tempered attitude. If there is no honey and self-discipline, the aggressive leader will become too demanding, boisterous in speech, lack self-control, and be pushy if results do not meet their standards. Although they are great for getting things started, taking charge, moving people along within their team, and are highly productive, the organization will suffer turnover, good employees will be driven away, and low morale and productivity will take place.

Having balanced and tempered leaders there is a higher probability to have longevity, great success, lasting and fruitful impact, and lead an influential power due to excellent work.

Walking In Excellence

Diligently making the switch from perfectionism to being a lady and leader of excellence, requires your attitude, character, output, speech, actions, and standard to align. I found myself being perfectly fine with mis-

Chapter 6 Excellence

takes and saw them as moments to learn and grow. At this stage of life I was humble enough to identify the mistakes and make an assertive effort to correct them. I am a firm advocate of one taking responsibility for their actions or mistakes because that demonstrates a person's character and integrity. Being a lady of excellence, it did not matter if someone noticed my efforts, integrity, standards, or character, I made up my mind a long time ago that others were not going to determine my behavior.

My worth and the way I thought and behaved were no longer tied to the expectation of other people, modern day times, culture norms in our society, sexism, or any other ism. Sexism is still a challenge as it was in former days that most women know all too well. Being a lady and leader of excellence is a lifestyle not just merely a means to getting a leadership position. Excellence is in every area of your life and it pulls you to be conscious, diligent, and put forth a consistent effort and attitude.

Seeking to be successful as a mom, leader, business owner, and in life as a whole was always my goal. However, I remembered my home life was out of order in the past and partly because I didn't care about the means. I was not focusing on doing things with excellence but perfection. I was charging after a concept I could not reach and I pushed many relationships to the breaking point and my marriage was a total loss. In this position, I did not run from the reality, the failure, but I learned to walk in excellence and identify the areas I fell short. Before I could fully walk in excellence I had to do my part to help bring restoration to the walls within my household that were damaged.

Are you involved with multiple programs, projects, present on several boards, that has your time stretched thin? When we are in a hurry we have less time for mistakes and problems to arise because we are already thinking of how this is stopping what is to come next. If mistakes bother you to the point where you are combative, you likely have too much on your plate. You may need to pull back on some things to get rest and bring healing where it is needed most.

I remember I was involved with a lot of different things for ministry and work that allowed to take my time and attention away from my family. When I was married, my ex-husband told me during our marriage I was involved in too much and it was not good or healthy. He tried to get me to see the I was out of balance and how it was negatively affecting our marriage and family. It was true, my family was suffering while I was out doing this and doing that for work, various projects in the community, volunteering at events, and doing ministry. I was doing good but bad at the same time by neglecting my family in the process.

The concept of work-life balance was not on my mind and I did not know how to slow down due to my ambitious mindset and drive. When I would be home, I would sometimes bring work home and not be fully present. My oldest son was a younger child at the time and he would speak to me about various things that were on his mind. If I did not respond in our conversation, he would ask mom are you listening? To be quite honest, I was half listening if that much because I would be distracted by doing something else at the same time.

Chapter 6 Excellence

Are you spinning multiple plates on sticks and barely there when people are around you. Do you have your mind chasing your next to-do list and are not listening to your 9-year-olds complaints about life? It is easy to assume you can multitask and not be attentive if you feel like what you are doing is more important. As queen multitasker, I have spent most of my life juggling housework , going to work, volunteering at church, and chasing starting and running my business. I have learned recently in the last couple of years, I needed to become less of a multitasker with my family and be more present in the house and in conversation.

After my divorce, I did a lot of self-examination and self-reflection when I began the venture of excellency. I purpose in my heart being to be excellent in every way possible and not settle for less. Making a decision to be and walk in excellence first in my home brought forth the fruit and blessing of healing and restoration to my relationship with my children. As we ladies walk in the spirit of excellence in every area, we will bring and add value to the table, be a change agent, and be able to make a difference in the lives of others. Being an excellent communicator is a quality I continuously work on graciously as I grow and develop. I encourage every leader to do the same in order to have a long shelf life in your sphere of influence and life.

Lead by Example

Great leaders I got the opportunity to hear from have emphasized the importance of leading with excellence and integrity as part of their foundation and leadership style. Over the years I have gained great wisdom and insight from different leaders I was led by and some I am still privileged to work with as my mentor. Mentors are a great value and if you have one in your life, be sure to appreciate them. Peer advisors, or accountability partners are also a great asset. I function as both for my clients because we all need someone who is neutral to be honest and not allow their love for us to cloud their vision of what they see. I learned how to be an effective leader by following helpful leaders who lead by example.

If you want to know how to find a leader, mentor, or accountability partner, start looking at how they live. What have they accomplished, and determine if you want the same or similar outcome. The strengths I saw exhibited in great leaders made them successful. It is not uncommon to have more than one leader, especially for different aspects of your life. You don't go to a dentist and ask them about your hair. You don't go to people who have no experience with your problem to request a solution. That is not to mean people who haven't walked in your shoes in that area cannot bring value, they can, but they would be presenting a different vantage point than your own.

Having a different perspective is great because it helps you to better understand people and see how you are perceived by others. I believe both points are valuable. I would put both leaders into my tool kit and apply their insight when the right problem arises. I do think having a leader that can relate to your unique personality and character is key to you feeling comfortable about making changes. Leading by example is a personal conviction of mine.

Chapter 6 Excellence

It is important as a conscious leader you are aware that people are watching your decision-making style, character, and your response in various moments, situations, and crises to see how well you handle them. Most people on your team will pay attention to their leader's actions that align with their words. Your actions get more results than your words alone ever could. Leading by example is modeling positive and healthy behavior, staying committed to your word, walking in integrity publicly and privately and displaying balance between work and your personal life.

An area that has yielded great success for me in leadership occurs when I pitch in to assist or work in a team effort. No one was to accomplish something major alone. You want the help of advisors, cheerleaders, and helpers to get you through. For every graduate you can show me from college, I can point to the team that helped them get there.

Although I am a girly girl, I never shied away from getting my hands dirty when the moment demands it because I am a team player. It takes a team to successfully build and sustain bountiful greatness both personally and professionally. No one person can do everything, we need one another in life.

As a mom and a leader, I have not asked my children or someone at work to do something I would not do, in my eyes that is leading by example. True leadership demonstrates leading by example and getting involved and not just barking instructions for others to follow. Personally speaking, when I was not in a leadership position, I sincerely appreciated and worked hard for leaders who got involved if they were physically able. Not to say I slacked off if the opposite was true, but the motivation would be different! Leaders that lead by example and excellency set themselves as the standard. Their willingness and ability to roll up their sleeves and get their hands dirty to help ensure the work gets done as planned makes an impact on people.

The Virtue Honeybee Lady avoids creating a culture of double standards. Her value for leading by example, integrity, and honesty are a high priority. Therefore, she will not be one that contradicts herself because that would create division. Anytime there is division with any team or culture if left unchecked, it will eventually crumble. According to Amy Rigby from Fingerprint for Success she stated, "Activate according to your values will set the right example for people to follow and will encourage those who may not have followed your lead before to take another note of the example you set."

As a leader, you control the culture and set the tone for how others value the mission, clients, and treat objectives. If you want your team to operate with integrity, you must operate in integrity. If you want a staff that will admit to faults and be accountable, you also have to demonstrate those values. As a leader if you make a mistake it is best to quickly own up to it, make it right, and display your leadership and expectations of them. Leadership is not just about control but responsibility.

Chapter 6 Excellence

Declaration for Excellence

I decree and declare as a Virtue Queen Honeybee Lady,

- I am an excellent leader who leads by example.
- I will lead with integrity, empathy, and excellence.
- As a Virtue Honeybee Lady I am balanced with work and life.
- I will continue to strive for excellence in every area of life.
- I move in the spirit of excellence and the fruit of great success will be evident from generation to generation.
- I will be an effective leader in my home and in the marketplace.
- My attitude, standards, character, actions, and words will reflect the spirit of excellence and the honey within me will flow out.
- I will establish a culture of excellence by leading with effective leadership and being an example.
- As a Virtue Honeybee Lady who walks in excellence, I will experience longevity, influence, and power to make an effective mark on this generation and the next generation.

Chapter 7 Serve

"Who is more important, the one who sits at the table or the one who serves? The one who sits at the table of course. But not here! For I am among you as one who serves"
Luke 22:27 NLT

If you had to point to your earliest leader that you loved and respected, who would that person be? I would argue that person would be your mother, a likely Virtue Honeybee Lady. Your mother, parent, or mother figure is the first person that shows you love and guidance. They are givers and share with you selflessly.

This leads me to a confirmed truth that the greatest among all people and leaders are the ones that serve. Great leaders are selfless and put the well-being, growth, development, and success of those they are called to lead and influence

Chapter 7 Serve

before their personal goals and ambition. History has regarded Rev. Dr. Martin Luther King Jr., Nelson Mandela, Sojourner Truth born Isabella Baumfree, Susan B. Anthony, Abraham Lincoln, Harriet Tubman, and W.E.B. Du Bois as phenomenal leaders given their character. These leaders exemplified prudence, empathy, foresight, awareness, vision, humility, courage, listening, accountability, compassion, integrity, and empowerment.

Going back as far as I can remember, I have had a heart to serve and volunteer. Serving to me is a way to give back and help others accomplish their goals. Service is the action of helping or doing work for someone: an act of assistance according to the Encyclopedia. A Virtue Queen Honeybee lady is a leader who serves and believes in servanthood. She serves her husband if married, children if she has any, family, community, her church, and her clients.

I remember in my early teens, I was a member of a small church that would give out monthly groceries to families in the community that came to the church. I would assist with putting all the items in the boxes early in that morning before we would start handing them out. The gratitude on the people's faces that showed up brought this little teenage girl much joy. I believe that is when servanthood was birthed out of me and I learned how to encourage others with positive words.

At first, I would offer a big warm smile when greeting people as I passed out the boxes. When I first started volunteering and connecting with people, I was nervous. Then after some time, a few words of encouragement would come out of my mouth. Noticing the impact of the few encouraging words, I was inspired to talk more and keep serving. My passion I wanted to share with my friends and I wanted them to experience what I had on Saturday mornings.

True leaders lead even without the title. When you are doing the right things it is natural to invite others to follow a good thing. Helping others by preparing these boxes of groceries and passing them out was my first leadership opportunity. Unbeknownst to me as a teenager I was being trained and conditioned to serve and be one that led my peers by example.

I thoroughly enjoy serving so much that I found myself involved in different things in the community. The heart to serve and be of service has been extremely important to me. Before I was able to become an effective leader leading in excellence, I had to learn to serve. Service does give you a heart for leadership. Desiring to serve others can be sparked in various ways, but I needed to repair and completely remove hindrance to reach my fullest potential.

Oftentimes, before anything new can come into our lives the old has to go because it is taking up space. If that space is in your closet, rooms in your home, space in your heart or mind, we get to a point where we need to take inventory and clean out what we do not need. For example, if you buy new living room furniture and the old furniture is still in place you will either have to move the old furniture to a new location or you may have to get rid of it completely. Once those things were removed doors opened for me to enter roles of leadership in the marketplace.

When I discovered the benefits of implementing ser-

Chapter 7 Serve

vant attitude, strategic transformation took place and my coaching style of leadership became fruitful and softened me. Prior to transforming myself, I believe I had more of a charismatic authority and visionary style of leadership. I am strong-willed, so when my mind is made up and I see the vision, I move full steam ahead with no looking back. Now I consider myself a balanced combination of those leadership styles as a virtue honeybee that learned when to employ each style as the moment demands.

A dynamic part to you and also your leadership style, is there is not just one approach you can take. We are dynamic people with varied experiences, skills, and talents. Do not feel you have to throw something away as you grow, you simply elevate and see how and if you can use it to get where you are going. Also of note, All leadership styles have their advantages and disadvantages. It is best to know your leadership style, remain open to growing and evolving as a leader, not be married to one particular style, and add honey to your style for balance. Bringing honey so you are not overly aggressive is important not just in leadership but also in relationships.

In the previous chapter, I mentioned the value and the importance of a team. Great leaders need a great team around them that support the vision and arrive to work daily to do their part to help the vision manifest. The days of being a lone ranger are long gone, you need a team. This team would help to build, problem solve, brainstorm, and increase productivity to name a few. It has been proven when a leader cultivates and empowers her team, people will be motivated to perform at a high level. The leader is building up her team's confidence by encouraging them, creating a safe environment, building trust, and empowering them to do their task.

What spheres of influence are you leading with excellence? It doesn't have to be limited to work, but can include people within your home, at your church, or during other activities. Becoming or nurturing this type of leader is strategic for any wise and savvy business. The soft and savvy leader knows how to engage, inspire, and encourage personal growth and development to increase employee engagement, lift levels of job satisfaction, help reduce stress, build healthy relationships, and establish a positive work culture. In addition, in her style of leadership, she inspires her team to be accountable for their part in the overall success of the business or company's objectives.

According to Pete Hinojosa's "Leadership Style: Balancing Results vs. Relationship" he stated, "Balance leadership requires that managers get to know their team members enough to understand what motivates each person, without this basic understanding you'll likely miss key opportunities to deliver the leadership they need in any given situation." The leader that makes this type of diligent observation and does something with the information is serving her team and the people around her. Success will chase her down because she is uncovering secrets to what makes a great influential leader in the making.

What are your thoughts? Do you feel a woman making use of these tools is no longer a common leader doing ordinary things, but a Virtue Honeybee leader? In recent years, I have applied this same understanding and principle n in relationships with the opposite sex. I learned

Chapter 7 Serve

to observe because oftentimes we speak before we listen and judge before we fully perceive what is happening. People's actions speak louder than their words, so sometimes we have to say less.

In observing, I got to know the person more. It didn't take months or years to discover exactly where a person was emotionally, spiritually, or otherwise. I also learned how best I could change to align myself with the man I wanted compared to who I was attracting at the time. I had to be coached, and renewed in how I interacted with the opposite sex. My prior experience was toxic to say the least, so much of what I learned was insufficient for the marriage I desire.

In my former days when I spoke my mind boldly without thinking it through, I was pushy and overly aggressive admittedly. In that past life I would not have taken the time to observe or study any man–not even my husband in an effort to build a healthy relationship. To be honest I probably would have been offended at the notion and would have thought to myself that responsibility falls solely on the man. Over the years, however, I have acquired greater understanding that has helped me produce flourishing relationships.

Women that are too independent struggle in the area of intimate relationships due to lack of cultivation. In other words she is not putting in the necessary work on her side when serving the relationship especially if she wants the long term. This is not to say men do not have a part to play. They are the ones that should do the chasing and pursuing while we as Virtue Honeybee Ladies decide to participate for the right one.

Shantay Adams

I know, I am going to get flak about being traditional. I know in modern day society there are some women that are stepping into the man's role and pursuing men. I have been there in the past truthfully speaking, before I knew and understood my worth and before I was healed, whole, and restored. Pursuing men can underline a more aggressive nature when approaching the opposite sex. Being so forward not only can shape your personality, but the reception of the man. People tend to appreciate what they work for and not what comes easily.

Now, I encourage my generation and the next generation coming behind me not to pursue a man but allow yourself to be presented. I am not saying women cannot speak or engage in conversation first, but we should not lead the realtionship's direction. I believe, again from a traditional view, a Virtue Honeybee Lady deserves to be treated as a lady. Ladies are meant to be taken care of, provided for, and watched over. This is not to say, women cannot contribute financially and other means, but that women have a role in a relationship as traditionally defined as help meet.

If you are desiring to enter a relationship and are currently single, I would like to share my experience. If a man who says he is interested in you and does not pursue you, I would use caution. Charging forward is invading their space and would mean you are putting more effort in than what you may get out.I had the privilege of entering a room on the Social Media platform Clubhouse, and the people on the stage were discussing women that pay for a man's travel to see her. The men said in agreement, those women are pursuing a man who doesn't have a serious interest in them.

Chapter 7 Serve

They continued to speak and some men on the stage began to laugh and did not mind if women were pursuing them in that way. As a bystander in the room for a brief time, I said this discussion ties into what I am currently writing about in this chapter. The timing was impeccable! As I have listened and heard mature, healed, and whole men say currently and in the past they like to do the chasing and they do not like women to pursue them, I felt compelled to share. If a man wants a woman he will make it known to her as she is presented.

"And the rib which the Lord God had taken from the man He made (fashioned, formed) into a woman, and He brought her and presented her to the man. Then Adams said, "this is now bone of my bones, and flesh of my flesh; she shall be called Woman because she was taken out of man." (Genesis 2:22-23 AMP)

I have learned that when a lady is presented to the man, if he is interested not only will he pursue and chase, but he will also make an investment. The right one is the one who is a purpose partner. What you both bring to the table should compliment each other's purpose in life. In this healthy pursuit, there would be no competition, but love, support, and mutual respect. I understand in some cultures and generations that might not be important but it is to be intentional and purposeful who you want to be in a committed relationship and marriage.

After my divorce and several years as a single lady, I learned what is important in a relationship and how to maintain a relationship without compromising my core values, beliefs, or lowering my standards. The overly aggressive independent woman that I was did not work for the purpose partner design. I didn't know it at the time, but I was self-sabotaging my future.

For those that are single or dating, my advice is to continue to cultivate and truly love you. Loving yourself, investing and working on serving you the best way, prepares you to love someone else while cultivating your confidence. If these steps are not firmly put in place any new relationship will start off on a shaky and sand-like foundation that if a strong wind comes along, the relationship will fall apart.

Having been married, I do have some life experience that I think is worthy to share. No marriage is perfect and they all have something that comes along to challenge the couple. The challenge can be with the intent to make one or both better in a given area. If you are married, and desire to stay married, it may mean making changes. I know there is a lot said about changing yourself for someone else; but getting better is not a bad compromise.

It took me years and ultimately a divorce for me to realize that I had needed to make necessary changes to my attitude and my overly aggressive and controlling personality. If I had made these adjustments prior to the divorce, the marriage could have had a better chance to succeed. With my mindset, I was not willing to do everything I could have to make my marriage work. I was not willing to make changes, but instead, I was focused on being right. I would share the advice, if you have a spouse that is working to be with you and showing they love and care about you, try to do everything you can also demonstrate your efforts.

Chapter 7 Serve

A husband that loves his wife, will tell her the hard truth even if she may not want to hear if she needs it. As a husband, his job is to care for you and help you live your purpose, and vice versa. Marriage is a team arrangement and you both win or lose collectively. When I realized it was not just about me, being right or getting my way, was when I acquired a marriage mindset. Being married, having a ceremony, or exchanging rings does not prepare you for marriage. Marriage is a heart commitment, a mind commitment, and an emotional commitment by both parties.

The Virtue Queen Honeybee lady is a woman that is single, married, employed, a business owner, or a career driven woman with or without children. We are women from different walks of life, experiences, and leadership know-how. One thing certain, before we can lead others and love others, we need to love and embrace ourselves. When we learn to release the honey from within, we can bring sweetness to those around us.

When an influential leader puts on the selfless invisible apron to serve, she gains followers because she understands the value in serving and how it will benefit all parties. Building relationships by investing in people is essential to having a strong influence as a leader. Caring and helping others does not imply the leader does the work, but she gives them information and guidance for them to complete their work successfully. Leaders are also serving when they educate others through mentorship, offering a course leading by example, and providing helpful tips that will help others accomplish their goals.

Shantay Adams

The more the Virtue Honeybee Lady releases the honey within her and serves, she will help bring out the best in others and inspire them to greater heights. Serving is a great key to foster effective communication, loyalty, and long lasting success. Being a lady of virtue in the workplace, you release honey in your workplace. She will ensure her environment is productive and has a culture of positivity. She cares about who is around her and how they are progressing. Let's face it, we are as good as our weakest link.

My sons like to share with me current events through Tik Tok, particularly my youngest son. He will either show me or send a text message of at least three or four videos a week. However, this new current event came from my oldest son who shared with me about an employee of a tech company that made a million dollar mistake. He thought he was going to lose his job when he was called in a meeting with leadership. The meeting lasted about two hours while there the meeting leader asked," *How did it occur?" "What did he learn? and "Do you know how to fix the problem?* The man said. "Yes", the leader got up and shook his hand and replied, "Okay, go back to work and fix it. I invested a million dollars in you and you know how to fix the problem."

As women, especially as Virtue Honeybee Ladies, we are capable of making mistakes. None of us are perfect, so don't beat yourself up if you make a mistake no matter how large. If you give yourself the same grace the boss gave this tech genius, you are open to growth. Making mistakes is a part of life as I suggested, but they are also growing opportunities that we cannot avoid. The same

Chapter 7 Serve

way you treat yourself or you want others to treat you, lead by example. Lead yourself and others with transformational leadership.

What happens when you lead with a transformational heart, gratitude can spring forth. I believe the employee who walked out of the meeting had a strong sense of gratitude but also a high motivation to be productive and perform well as a leader. You can turn your challenges, mistakes, into motivation. Don't be so quick to discard your mistakes as disadvantages or think mistakes always have to equal loss. They can be a big win to your motivation, confidence, and build relationships.

A few years ago, I was volunteering for different facilities that were teaching and feeding the homeless at my local downtown library. At the time I was inspired by Larry Devereaux (Coach), and his style of leadership. He saw the gifts and talents within me and gave me an opportunity to grow in the area of teaching. He helped cultivate and encourage the honey deep within me to come out from within me and then pour it out like a drink offering that is sweet like honeycomb for the benefits of others. He was of course not the only coach I have had that has made an impact on my life. There have been others that have come alongside me in recent years that have helped me become a better version of me. I want to let you know, it is okay for you to have more than one influence. Be sure to diversify your influencers to meet the demands on your life.

I want to leave you with this powerful quote from John Maxwell saying, "The first step to leadership is servanthood". The Leader that adopts this mindset and character will see fruitful, profitable, and bountiful success. I am grateful for the experience I gained as a teenager serving and volunteering in the community. I loved given back and honestly I became a coach, speaker, and now author to do more to help more ladies with problems I too faced. It is a ongoing battle to keep the right mind and I realized I can be a help to someone else like I received. I want to pass it forward and I am starting with you.

My deepest hope and expectation is that you found this book to serve as a blessing and benefit to you. As a lady and leader in your home and in the marketplace, I trust you will be open and willing to release the honey within you. No looking back, no shrinking back, to old habits you say "good-bye" and "hello future!" Now, get up and rise to the occasion of who you were always designed to be in this world. I exhort you to walk boldly, fearlessly, audaciously, courageously, and unapologetically as a Virtue Queen Honeybee Lady.

Chapter 7 Serve

Declaration for Serve

I decree and declare as *a Virtue Queen Honeybee Lady,*

- I believe in servanthood with excellence.
- I will cultivate, build, and serve my team with relationship-based leadership resulting in oriented culture.
- I will remain open and balanced in my leadership style.
- I will boldly, courageously, and fearlessly be a leader that stands out in my act of service in leadership that will cause me to be effective & influential.
- At home, my household will prosper, be fruitful, profitable, and have long-lasting success.
- In my business, I will prosper, be fruitful, profitable, and have long-lasting success.
- In the workplace, I will prosper, be fruitful, profitable, and have long-lasting success.
- I will cultivate, serve, invest in me unapologetically.

Affirmations

Chapter 1:
- That will produce honey which is generating success, effectiveness, abundance, wealth, influence, and sustainability in life and leadership.
- I have value and worth inside of me that I bring to the table.
- I walk in Wisdom and Understanding, life, grace, and favor will be with me in my life, household, career, business, and marriage.
- I will empower my generation and the next generation to know they have value and worth inside of them.
- I will be balanced in being soft and savvy.
- I will walk discipline with a daily diet of honey.
- I will start what I finish boldly and courageously.
- That loves and invest in myself. I will grow and

Affirmations

evolve into a better version of me.
- I will be an authentic, unique, and distinguished Virtue Honeybee Lady in life and leadership.
- I am brave, virtuous, humble, confident, intelligent, temper, gentle, bold, resilient, resolute, peaceful, wise, beautiful inside and out, calm, strong, excellent, and ladylike.

Chapter 2:
- As a Virtue Queen Honeybee Lady, I will walk in my authentic unapologetic true identity because I am fully acquainted with myself.
- In this world I know who I am and where I am going as I walk purposefully.
- No matter the situation or circumstances, I will walk boldly and courageously in my true self as I was originally designed without shrinking back, but rise to every occasion set before me.
- I will be balanced as being soft and savvy as a Virtue Honeybee Lady and leader that will cause success, healthy relationships, prosperity, and wealth.
- I will consistently implement a work-life balance scale to avoid burnout.
- Walking in my unapologetic true identity will impact and influence this generation and the next generation of ladies to live and walk in their authentic identity unapologetically.
- As a Virtue Honeybee Lady, I will maintain a healthy balance in life as a whole and get proper rest to steer clear of deficiencies and ineffectiveness.
- I will walk in full grown love as a Virtue Honeybee Lady that expels all kinds of fear.
- My identity is not tied to my accomplishments, validation, or approval from others, but who I am as a

lady and leader.

Chapter 3:
- I am restored and have returned back to my original state and condition as a virtue queen honeybee lady.
- I am restored in my mind and thoughts as a thought leader due to restoration.
- I am not a creativity killer; I am restored back to creativity and innovation.
- As a result of allowing restoration to occur in my life, I have been restored to increase, greatness, enlargement, beautification, blessings, prosperity, and success is my portion.
- Creative strategies and ideas will flow out of me because I am restored
- My business, enterprises, company, organization, household, family, marriage, ministry, shall blossom and grow exponentially due to restoration.
- I decree and declare uncommon favor, joy, peace, life, strength, and good health will come to me because of restoration.
- Every broken down wall in my life and around my life as a leader will be restored due to restoration.
- There will no longer be imbalance in loyalty, I have healthy boundary lines that I will honor because of restoration.
- I embrace restoration to be soft and savvy is my portion.

Chapter 4:
- I am tactful.
- I am an influential tactful leader that provides first class service and leadership.
- I will use prudence and wisdom from above in my

actions and speech because I understand the art of tactfulness and diplomacy.
- I will aim to preserve peace and be tactful in my response and approaches with the right timing and tone.
- I will be a successful leader in every area that I am called to lead or co-lead and the fruit will be evident.
- As an influential leader, my walls are strong and healthy because I walk in true humility and willingness to serve others.
- My name will go before me in rooms I have not yet entered because I am a Virtue Queen Honeybee that has a good name and reputation as one who is tactful, uses mindfulness and diplomacy as a leader.
- I have a healthy emotional intelligence IQ.

Chapter 5:
- I will walk as an unstoppable influential Virtue Honey bee Lady.
- I will remain courageous, fearless, bold, and audacious as an unstoppable leader in my personal and professional life.
- I will remain resilient and resolute as an unstoppable leader who refuses to quit.
- I will lead with integrity and empathy to help ensure great success.
- I will honor the vision given to me along with my "why" and go forth unstoppably.
- I will continue to adopt the *"I can"* and *"I will overcome"* attitude in my personal and professional life.
- I will flourish as an unstoppable influential leader who will effectively impact this world.
- I will do phenomenal things as a leader in leadership as I remain unstoppable.

Chapter 6:
- I am an excellent leader who leads by example.
- I will lead with integrity, empathy, and excellence.
- As a Virtue Honeybee Lady I am balanced with work and life.
- I will continue to strive for excellence in every area of life.
- I move in the spirit of excellence and the fruit of great success will be evident from generation to generation.
- I will be an effective leader in my home and in the marketplace.
- My attitude, standards, character, actions, and words will reflect the spirit of excellence and the honey within me will flow out.
- I will establish a culture of excellence by leading with effective leadership and being an example.
- As a Virtue Honeybee Lady who walks in excellence, I will experience longevity, influence, and power to make an effective mark on this generation and the next generation.

Chapter 7:
- I believe in servanthood with excellence.
- I will cultivate, build, and serve my team with relationship-based leadership resulting in oriented culture.
- I will remain open and balanced in my leadership style.
- I will boldly, courageously, and fearlessly be a leader that stands out in my act of service in leadership that will cause me to be effective & influential.
- At home, my household will prosper, be fruitful, profitable, and have long-lasting success.

Affirmations

- In my business, I will prosper, be fruitful, profitable, and have long-lasting success.
- In the workplace, I will prosper, be fruitful, profitable, and have long-lasting success.
- I will cultivate, serve, invest in me unapologetically.

About the Author

Shantay Adams is a dynamic speaker, coach, mentor, consultant, HR professional, and minister. She has experienced great transformation in her own life and desire to walk with other ladies to help bring forth greater transformation in their lives. She believes in walking in her true identity unapologetically and walking in her purpose.

Shantay has a passion for coaching women and especially helping women who struggle with being overly aggressive. As a coach and speaker, Shantay has a powerful message that helps ladies who are overly committed, loyal, and passionate about helping others to a fault become balance.

Striving for excellence is the primary goal that will help

About the Author

ladies that are leaders resist the temptation of perfectionism. Shantay is lifting up her voice to remind them they are loved and valuable. With a unique style and delivery, Shantay disarms even the most aggressive women by being soft and savvy. You can catch more with honey, and get more done with a soft but firm and loving word.

Shantay Adams is the Business Owner & CEO of Fresh New Consulting, a coaching and consulting company. She offers courses, programs and workshops to help professionals and women add honey to achieve greater success.

To book Shantay, learn more, or reserve coaching services, scan the below:

Shantay Adams

It's time to start and finish **YOUR Story**!

KLE Publishing specializes in helping people become authors. In as little as 15 to 90 days, we can help you develop your book and publish to 39,000 outlets!

Ghostwrite, Edit, Format, Publish
We can help from
Start to Finish.

KLEPub.com Store

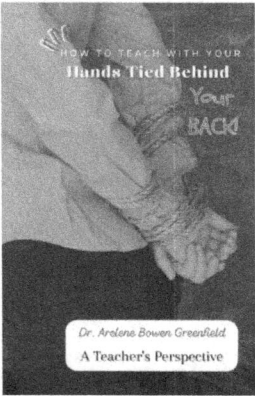

www.ingramcontent.com/pod-product-compliance
Lightning Source LLC
Chambersburg PA
CBHW062141280426
43673CB00072B/84